Joy (Or Something Darker, but Like It)

POETS ON POETRY

Derek Pollard, Series Editor
Donald Hall, Founding Editor

For a complete list of titles, please see www.press.umich.edu

Joy (Or Something Darker, but Like It)

poetry & parenting

Essays

NATHANIEL PERRY

University of Michigan Press
Ann Arbor

For questions or permissions, please contact um.press.perms@umich.edu

Published in the United States of America by the
University of Michigan Press
Manufactured in the United States of America
Printed on acid-free paper
First published July 2024
A CIP catalog record for this book is available from the British Library.

Library of Congress Cataloging-in-Publication data has been applied for.

ISBN 978-0-472-03971-5 (paper : alk. paper)
ISBN 978-0-472-22178-3 (e-book)

"Gentlemen, the Bicycles Are Coming!" from *101 Different Ways of Playing Solitaire and Other Poems* by Belle Randall, ©1973. Reprinted by permission of the University of Pittsburgh Press. All other poems by Belle Randall reprinted by permission of the author.

"A Cold Spring," "Sandpiper"; excerpt from "Filling Station" from POEMS by Elizabeth Bishop. Copyright © 2011 by The Alice H. Methfessel Trust. Publisher's Note and compilation copyright © 2011 by Farrar, Straus and Giroux. Reprinted by permission of Farrar, Straus and Giroux. All Rights Reserved.

Excerpts from "The Pentecost Castle," "Lachrimae," and "Hymns to Our Lady of Chartres" from *Broken Hierarchies* by Geoffrey Hill, ed. Kenneth Haynes, ©2014. Reproduced with the permission of Oxford Publishing Limited through PLSclear.

"Evening" from *Tellico Blue* by George Scarbrough, ©1949. Reproduced with the permission of the George Scarbrough Center, Reinhardt University.

"The Source is Anywhere" from *Summer So-Called* by George Scarbrough, ©1956. Reproduced with the permission of the George Scarbrough Center, Reinhardt University.

Primus St. John, "A Poem to My Notebook, Across Winter," "Lyric 12," "Lyric 13," and excerpts from "Dreamer" and "If There Were No Days" from *Communion: New and Selected Poems.* Copyright © 1999 by Primus St. John. Reprinted with the permission of The Permissions Company, LLC on behalf of Copper Canyon Press, coppercanyonpress.org.

"Astronauts". ©1978 Robert Hayden, from *Collected Poems of Robert Hayden* by Robert Hayden, edited by Frederick Glaysher. Used by permission of Liveright Publishing Corporation.

Excerpts from "The Womanhood ['The Children of the Poor,' 'Life for my child is simple, and is good,' 'The Ballad of the Light-Eyed Little Girl (16 lines)']" by Gwendolyn Brooks from *Blacks*, ©1987. Reprinted by consent of Brooks Permissions.

"Pastoral" from *Country Poems* by Elizabeth Coatsworth, ©1942. Reprinted by the kind permission of Elizabeth Gartner.

Also by Nathaniel Perry: *Nine Acres* and *Long Rules: An Essay in Verse*

Contents

Contents

Acknowledgments

Versions of some of the essays in this book first appeared in *American Poetry Review, Kenyon Review, Fourth Genre,* and *Michigan Quarterly Review.* Many thanks to the editors of these journals.

Thanks to Derek Pollard, Elizabeth Demers and the rest of the staff at the University of Michigan Press for believing in this project and helping me imagine it into life.

I'd like mostly just to thank my children—Horatio, Jane Bell and Lois—for letting me write about them. I hope they'll think I did it right and well. And, of course, nothing about this book would have been possible without my amazing wife, and partner in all things, Kate, without whom I would not be a parent, a poet, or probably much of anything at all.

Breathing and Interested

The Bequests of Edward Thomas
(2015)

I want to tell you a story about my daughter Jane Bell. Not too long ago, she was nearly five at the time, we were walking to get the mail. Our driveway is long—about two-fifths of a mile from the house to the mailbox—so it is a substantial hike for someone with short legs, but the kids are always game for it. Well, the time I'm referring to now it was just me and Rache (our oldest) and Jane Bell headed down to the mail on a chilly windy day. The clouds hung overhead like a fixture with a bulb out, not looming or menacing, but something still to notice. What JB had noticed, though, was beneath the clouds: a crow and a vulture sort of circling one another. Now, I know these birds don't usually interact, unless they are bickering over the same carcass, but to Jane Bell, they were engaged in some sort of skydance.

I asked her what she was looking at and she replied, "I'm watching the crows. They're interesting."

I didn't really know how to respond—by telling her they weren't both crows? By pointing out that most people don't look twice at crows or vultures? In the end I think I let her just have her moment. I would give a lot to know exactly what was passing through her head then, exactly what was "interesting."

After we made it to the mailbox (in it was some fabric for my wife's sewing business, clippings and stickers from a grandmother, a poetry journal, and ads), Janie immediately turned and started running back towards home with Rache on her heels. She didn't stop, and I saw her next in the house under a blanket eating a roll and waiting for me.

What I kept thinking about, as I walked the dogs back up the driveway in the cold wake of my kids who had disappeared back up over the hill, were all the times I have showed her, or any of them, something I thought was interesting, or something I thought they would think was interesting. Lots of times, I've been right, and they've marveled for a few respectful seconds and then run back to whatever they had been doing. Other times, they haven't even begun to care that much. But this crow thing, it was an interest of her own making and discovering. No one had told her to find it interesting; it wasn't suggested by YouTube or a science video at school. It was her eye composing the world. This is exactly what Emerson was talking about nearly two hundred years ago, and something a lot of us still easily can forget how to do.

I want to turn now to a poem, and to what anyone would consider a very unusual poem to think about in the context of parenting and intuition and the world. But in the context of the interest that Jane Bell suggested on our walk to the mailbox, I think it makes plenty of sense. This is a war poem by Edward Thomas and, I think, one of the most emotionally intense poems in English. It is certainly the best home front poem I know of. And Thomas, as Matthew Hollis's wonderful biography reminds us, was not only a great friend of Robert Frost's, but he was a dedicated father. He was in many ways a miserable man—constantly tortured by indecision (Frost's "The Road Not Taken" has Thomas explicitly and mockingly in mind), tortured by the ways his life did not match up to what he'd imagined, and tortured by his difficulties in providing for his family. But in all Thomas's poems, the knowledge of a father of young children is not far below the surface. I'm not trying to make a cloying biographical reading here, it wouldn't be there. But what is here is the same concept Jane Bell was getting at, and what her crows are getting at, of course. Let's look at the poem:

BLENHEIM ORANGES

Gone, gone again,
May, June, July,
And August gone,
Again gone by,

Not memorable
Save that I saw them go,
As past the empty quays
The rivers flow.

And now again,
In the harvest rain,
The Blenheim oranges
Fall grubby from the trees,

As when I was young—
And when the lost one was here—
And when the war began
To turn young men to dung.

Look at the old house,
Outmoded, dignified,
Dark and untenanted,
With grass growing instead

Of the footsteps of life,
The friendliness, the strife;
In its beds have lain
Youth, love, age, and pain:

I am something like that;
Only I am not dead,
Still breathing and interested
In the house that is not dark:—

I am something like that:
Not one pane to reflect the sun,
For the schoolboys to throw at—
They have broken every one.

I think we can read the first two stanzas here as describing the speaker's
own early life; so in our reading, a father's remembrance (or lack thereof)

of his own childhood. What he remembers, or claims to remember, is nothing but the passage of time—months. Except, of course, this is an adult's memory; children rarely think about months in the way we do. And he suggests this adult perspective with the simile that ends the second stanza (the familiar river of time). He then brings the poem back to the present with a natural image.

> In the harvest rain
> The Blenheim Oranges
> Fall grubby from the trees.

These "oranges," (Blenheim Oranges are really a cultivar of apple, used mostly in cooking), which should have been harvested by men, but are instead being harvested by rain, arrest the speaker into interest. Just like Jane Bell on our walk down the driveway, we feel the poem pause and turn as the speaker looks up to consider this image. It takes him right back to memory, which he now sees with slightly more detail—"As when I was young / And when the lost one was here." Notice too, as the interest takes hold, the rhyme scheme becomes less predictable as well. But what he remembers (the "lost one," a friend perhaps? someone not much older than a child?) brings him back to the more recent past—the beginning of the First World War.

As were all Edward Thomas's poems, this poem was written in the last few years of his life, before he was killed in the war, at Arras. So there is often something elegiac in the way we hear his voice (it was a time of vast cultural elegy as well), but this poem feels full too of the difficulty of preserving what little the world still seems to offer (those good apples gone grubby and untaken). With such a tone well-established, the poem moves to its main image; the deserted and broken-eyed house.

> Look at the old house,
> Outmoded, dignified,
> Dark and untenanted,

As is often the case with images in a poem, this one seems to have double meaning. After having described his somewhat empty memory of childhood in the early stanzas, the reader immediately connects the empty house to the speaker of the poem—"outmoded, dignified." This poem in its seemingly neatly rhymed quatrains is definitely dignified, and already, even in the late 1910s, maybe a little outmoded too. It is a poem spoken in a voice that is no longer that of a child (carefree, new) but it has been, at points, full of "youth, love, age and pain." But, not content with the simple metaphor, Thomas then draws the connection himself with his lucid refrain—"I am something like that;"

Only I am not dead,
Still breathing and interested
In the house that is not dark:—

And this is it—the moment where the poem explodes out of its historical moment and into the realm of universal human experience. The word "interested" would be the most noticeable word in the stanza even without its connection to the anecdote with which I began this essay. With its amazing ear-boggling rhyme with "dead," the word almost resurrects the dead in its off-ness. But it is also off in diction; it is a word that seems scientific almost, detached, observational or uncommitted. We expect, in this elegiac mode, on the heels of the 19th century, something more like "I pine" for the undarkened house, or I am "griefstricken" or who knows what. But "interested" throws the reader back on her heels. We are "breathing and interested," and that is a pretty solid definition of what it means to be alive. When Jane Bell looked up at those birds, she did not see a cold excluding sky, she did not complain immediately about the wintry wind puffing her hair out around the rim of her homemade hat, but she saw two black birds who, to her, were not dark. The world was enlightened by their presence—and she, though she may not have been able to put it into words, wanted to know how they did it. Or perhaps she just wanted to watch them do it. She was, suddenly, interested.

Now, I'll finish looking at the poem in a minute (I know we can't leave it off there without some fussing), but let's keep thinking about that word "interested." How do we cultivate this kind of interest? Both in our kids and in ourselves? Is it an interest that we can share? It is, I think, an awareness of paradox, an awareness of suddenly shifting expectations, an awareness, of course, of beauty, but also an awareness of the beauty of experience. I think, too, it is something we can practice. We keep a small group of chickens, whose numbers fluctuate based on the availability of laying hens in our area and the hunger and tenacity of our local hawks and owls. At the moment, we are down to only three hens and one rooster. Though we have so few, the hens are young and have audaciously laid eggs all through the winter, so they've been a real surprise. The rooster, as are many of his ilk, is a renowned jerk in our family, though he does admittedly do his job. He has of late been picking on the smaller of the hens—chasing her around, dominating her endlessly in the various ways that happens, and basically making me wonder if he knows something I didn't know, like if she was sick or hurt or something along those lines. Now you can't really take a chicken to the vet out here, so there's not much I can do if she were sick, but you still worry about any creature under your direct care, so I've been worrying.

When I went out to shut the coop last night, I noticed she wasn't in with the others, and I found her hunkered down in the leaves up by the edge of the fenceline. She saw me coming to check on her and hightailed it—as only a hen can do, with wild squawking and windmilling feet—into the coop. As I bent to look in the grated window on the back of the coop to see if I could get a better look at her, she popped her head up into the window, just inches from my nose. It so startled me, and the look on her face (if chickens compose their looks) was one of such wide-eyed surprise to see me there that I fell back laughing and laughing. Seconds after that I noticed from her rear feathers that she may indeed be a little sick, so I stopped my laughing and resumed my mild state of concern. However, it is that moment of laughter that gives me pause. What is that part of the mind that reacts to things how they ought to be reacted to, instead of always filtering observations through the context of the moment, or through what the mind has been engaged in prior to the moment? The hen's face was funny, and for a brief moment of relief, I found it funny.

It is easy to get mad at our kids when they lose focus or stop paying attention ten seconds after they promised they would give us their full attention. But it seems imperative to find a way to differentiate between lapses in focus, and the sudden onset of interest. Kids are, of course, interested in "the house that is not dark," because most of them (thankfully) have not had much experience with the dark kind. And even when they have, the light tends to dominate. But parents are often on the other side of that spectrum. We forget about the house with light, we have to remind ourselves, as Thomas reminds himself, that we are indeed "breathing" and still "interested." Thomas in fact, in the last stanza of the poem (which we *will* look at) tries to pull back from the power of that breathing self, but he doesn't fully leave it. The reader leaves the poem if not with hope, then with the awareness of awareness, which is certainly more than darkness. And we can keep this in mind with our kids. We have to be aware that they are aware of the world in flux, with all its sudden changes and paradoxes and moods.

The human world often seems, to us and to them, somehow controllable and predictable (though it really isn't of course). The natural world, or non-human world, or whatever you want to call it, though, is often the essence of interest. There are a thousand things to catch the eye—the hue of morning light laid up against a tree trunk, a flock of sparrows rising suddenly out of the bracken at the edge of the woods, a cardinal hopping and hunting in a patch of winter cover-grass, the surprising green of the pine, the bamboo someone improbably planted twenty years ago. We can notice these things, and we can notice our kids noticing them. We can then take this understanding of the peripatetic eye back in the house and be a little less judgmental when things shift suddenly, when interest moves our kids' minds (and our own minds) away from the moment.

And, weirdly, this can lead us to the end of the poem. Thomas repeats his refrain, now darkly considered:

I am something like that:
Not one pane to reflect the sun,
For the schoolboys to throw at—
They have broken every one.

Though this seems to pull us away from the hopefulness, or awareness at least, of our "breathing" and being "interested," it doesn't quite. The observation seems almost sort of a denouement in the poem, or a deflation of what it had previously given the reader. We are not surprised to see Thomas return to grief and the adult awareness of loss, but it does not undo the "interest" from the previous stanza. In my reading, in fact, it throws it into greater relief. The speaker is both "breathing and interested," *and* terrifically fractured and sad. I intimated in the last paragraph that this ending has something to do with being outside, and it seems significant that the poem stays *out* of the house. The speaker is indeed standing in the non-human world (or at least not under a roof) when he makes this final observation. His being interested, and outside, has allowed him to understand his contradictory but very human position—he is both alive and like the dead he is mourning. Maybe Jane Bell, though not thinking about death, was having a similar awareness of contradiction; the birds were not the same but were acting the same. The sky was grey, perhaps, but not the grey she'd expected. Who knows? She realized something almost unnamable, saw herself as part of a much larger thing, and was interested, breathing and alive.

Let's turn our discussion of Thomas to a poem he wrote for one of his daughters. I think it gets at this interest in the context of parenting a bit differently, and in perhaps a more direct way. It is the third poem in a suite of four "Household Poems," one written for each of his three children and one for his wife. This is the one for his youngest daughter:

MYFANWY

What shall I give my daughter the younger
More than will keep her from cold and hunger?
I shall not give her anything.
If she shared South Weald and Havering,
Their acres, the two brooks running between,
Paine's Brook and Weald Brook,
With pewit, woodpecker, swan, and rook,
She would be no richer than the queen
Who once on a time sat in Havering Bower
Alone, with the shadows, pleasure and power.
She could do no more with Samarcand,
Or the mountains of a mountain land
And its far white house above cottages
Like Venus above the Pleiades.
Her small hands I would not cumber
With so many acres and their lumber,
But leave her Steep and her own world
And her spectacled self with hair uncurled,
Wanting a thousand little things
That time without contentment brings.

I love this kind of poem—the sort that shatters all expectations from the very beginning. That third line—"I shall not give her anything"—is just so arresting and surprising, the reader reads on newly centered by what the poem has to say. This is a poem that doesn't focus on the "interest" of the first poem with as much clarity, but it is there beneath the surface of the poem's conclusions. So let's look at how Thomas gets there. After claiming he won't give his daughter anything, Thomas moves along to suggest all the things she might have had from him (and, since this is a poem, he, in a sense, is giving her anyway), which in this poem are mostly places and their non-human inhabitants. Thomas was a great walker and bicyclist—he knew enormous swaths of countryside and their country lanes by heart—and, for him, there maybe were no greater things than small sights like "Paine's Brook and Weald Brook, / with pewit, woodpecker, swan, and rook." The pair of proper nouns gives the little girl all at once both pain and wellness ("weald" being a forest, but "weal" meaning something like "well" or "good"), and the animals suggest the presence of life beyond and behind our human ones.

Now Thomas clearly loves these things. We can tell by the way he sets these named places and things in the context of the meter and rhyme of this poem[1]—so why not "give" them to his little daughter? Perhaps by withholding the names and places, Thomas hopes to keep awake in his daughter her native awareness of the world, to let her own original imagination name and dictate and become interested in the world around her. She will one day have these things and others like them, but perhaps she does not yet need them. He continues the poem by suggesting that these names, the beauty in these places, are indeed riches—the little girl becomes a kind of queen in the subsequent lines—but she is not a happy queen. She, with her future speculative human riches, is "Alone, with the shadows, pleasure and power." How different from the bird-encrusted brooks we just passed over. The poem then imagines as Myfanwy's gift the universe entire; it moves from England out to the near-east (all the exotic sand and silk and glitter of the place are captured by the single name of Samarcand) and then further out to some imagined kingdom of mountains and cottages with its lonely ruling "white house" and up to

1. Note, for instance, how, for this poem written in iambic tetrameter, the sixth line makes for an unusual metrical gesture indeed. One must read the names of those two creeks as containing two full stresses each to make metrical sense of the line. Thomas intends the reader to linger over these names and savor them.

the stars, where Venus rules in the image above the seven sisters of the darkened sky.

So he has both given her and not given her these things. They are given in language by being present in the poem, but are withheld as true gifts. They are gifts he has imagined giving her but has decided against. Why? Because he has a better gift for her. He will

> ... leave her Steep and her own world,
> And her spectacled self with hair uncurled,
> Wanting a thousand little things
> That time without contentment brings.

The image of home returns the girl to her innocence first off. She is no longer the sad queen from the earlier lines, but is again a quiet disheveled curious little girl (we read the curiosity in the metonym of those glasses perhaps). But in that innocence is also crucial knowledge—the knowledge of "her own world." Thomas was fully in love with his own world. As I said before, he knew the countryside and the country lanes and his country neighbors and probably individual trees better than most people know their friends. So this, for Thomas, was the ultimate gift—the thing you already have. It is important to notice that he does give that local world its name—Steep—reminding us again that language is important in shaping the world, but now it is a word that belongs too to his daughter and her imagination, which is, we presume, the true ruler of "her own world."

Thoreau and Emerson, of course, go on at great length about our need to travel in our own worlds, to locate the marvelous and wonderful in the grounds we find around us. In fact, the American nature writing tradition is full of this kind of exploration of what the poet George Scarbrough calls "the county world"—the near world, the personal world. But these writers almost exclusively talk about this kind of understanding of the world in the context of solitude, a single man or woman out exploring, understanding and composing the world. Edward Thomas, though, in this poem and in others, may be one of the few writers I can think of to link this kind of understanding of beauty and knowledge also to the role of the father or mother. Certainly the young Myfanwy here is a picture of semi-content solitude—but, like the house at the end of "Blenheim

Oranges," she is being watched. So Thomas takes up the classic stance of the parent—full of knowledge, and unsure how to give it to his child or not even sure if he wants or needs to give it to her.

Consider for a moment how the poem ends, again on a seemingly down note. The little girl sits uncontented and destined to remain in a world without contentment. But these lines, as in the first poem we looked at, make for more of a paradoxical ending than one might at first think. Haven't we just learned in the first half of the poem that the contentment of desires is either impossible or unwise? Little Myfanwy has already been the queen of the universe in this poem, and that contentment, that ultimate fulfillment did nothing to make her future self any less inquisitive or less needy for more knowledge, more names for the things she finds. So I think the parent has to read those last lines as not so much an indictment of his or her inability to find happiness for their children or to give it to them, but instead as a realization that somewhere in being unfulfilled *is* the chance at happiness. To always be needing to know more, to be always wondering what a bird is saying or where the pewit nests, is to be always trying to understand the world (never caring, Thomas suggests, if we own it or not). These "thousand little things" are not, in my reading, the smartphones and hair-bows and half-mocha caramel iced oat venti lattes of our contemporary world, but instead are more akin to the ten thousand things of Taoism, the (seemingly) little things that literally make the world—woodpeckers, rooks, pain, and Paine's Brook.

So Thomas, at the end of the poem, knows what all of us know—that the world is difficult and sad, and that we can never have enough of it. But he also knows that contained within that fact is all the joy of being in the world. We cannot prepare our children for what the world won't give them, but we can let them take what it will give them without getting in the way. I hope that is what I did for Jane Bell that day on the driveway. She hasn't mentioned the two birds since then—they did not bring her contentment I suppose, but they did bring her the knowledge of it. She was "interested," as Myfanwy clearly is at the end of Thomas' poem, and that in itself is enough. When you are interested in something, that interest almost assumes in its inception that you won't find out all that you want or need to know. When in the fall I kneel to inspect a flowering roadside weed, I learn nothing other than what my hands and eyes can tell me. But that is OK, or more than OK. I may even forget to look up the name later, but it is the interest in the moment that keeps me breathing, that keeps us moving through the world with our eyes open. I hope beyond anything else I can give her, that I can give that to Jane Bell, or leave her to it, more accurately. I hope she will not go to war like Thomas and so many of his friends, and I hope she will not become ensnared in the glittering constellations of material things she thinks she wants to have. But I can't stop her. I can instead, like Thomas in his beautiful poems, give her the want, the desire, to see those thousand good little things, and always be interested in them. And, god willing, I'll be breathing for a good long while beside her as she goes.

The Sound of a Door That Is Opened

Longfellow on Letting the Kids In
(2015)

One day when he was little, my son Horatio (he goes by Rache) came running out of what we call the Big Room in our house to tell me I had to come with him to Pirate Cove—a swale at the edge of our woods so named by a friend of ours who buccaneered frequently with the kids. He wanted to show me a tree he'd found. Our woods were bounded then by a clear-cut in its sixth year of recovery, so the sun came through loud and clear, and it nearly blinded me as I trotted eastward, keeping up with Rache zooming ahead. What he'd uncovered was a small stand of what I know is often called arrowwood (or Bursting Hearts or Strawberry Bush, or any number of other names), and he had seen it before with me on a walk one morning. But he didn't remember the name, only its ridiculously out-of-place glow-orange berries, and the wild and spiny lychee-like seed pod split open around them. He recognized the creativity of the thing before he thought about whatever we might need to call it. And I'm pretty sure he doesn't remember the name still (which it was given, of course, for the strength and flexibility of its wood, used by indigenous peoples to make arrow shafts, or for its ridiculous color, or for its imaginary sadness, or . . .), but has instead fixed in his mind the image and whatever name he has attached to it—glowbush, deer ice-cream, superberry, wildwood, pirate weed, etc.

This is a complicated moment—do I let him *into* the human world by rendering up to him the plant's name, which has its own comforts and pleasures to be sure, the comfort of shared knowledge and participation, or do I let him stay *out* in the prairies of his mind, where the image he has made has formed language of its own, where creativity and knowledge have for the moment become the same thing? I don't know the answer to this question, but I know that I was sort of shocked by the realization that the choice exists. And it exists again and again as we blindly parent along. Do we explain to kids that violence is sometimes necessary (and according to some games, fun), or do we let them have their visceral reactions of terror for as long as we can? Do you explain the ins and outs of whatever particular religion we might or might not subscribe to right away, or do you let them engage with their spiritual lives in a creative and questioning way? Can I do both? Again, there are obvious benefits to both approaches, and this essay is not a self-righteous screed, but instead, I hope, an essay advocating and exploring a kind of awareness that is easy not to foster.

John Keats, in a letter to a friend, famously espoused the idea of "negative capability," by which he means the ability to hold two opposed ideas in one's mind as being somehow equally true. Or that opposite truths do not negate one another, but instead enrich each other. There is an obvious eastern quality to this idea, and it was not new when Keats thought of it, but he says it perhaps the most simply. In referring to Shakespeare specifically, he writes that the ideal of Negative Capability exists when a person "is capable of being in uncertainties, mysteries, doubts, without any irritable reaching after fact and reason." So perhaps he doesn't only mean two opposing truths (though it is often construed that way), but instead any and all opposing truths. That "knowledge" should not be bound to context. Ten or so years later Ralph Waldo Emerson would get at something similar in his famous essay *Nature*, where he asks us to be creative and compositional observers of the natural world, "transparent eyeballs" as he terms it. Children, one could argue, are naturally philosophers in this way. But it is important to realize that we do need to encourage them not only to grow and age toward adulthood, but instead to retain some of that transparency as they make their way up and through the world.

Well, I thought for a while on Edward Thomas, which you begrudged me, and now in this chapter have mentioned a handful of other poets, so you may have guessed that I think in poetry there may be a model for this approach to parenting. I don't think I'm saying that we should always look to poets as model parents (ahem), but instead that in the way art works on us, the ways in which poems work on us, we might find something to learn about engaging with our children. Here's a well-loved poem by the overly-maligned Henry Wadsworth Longfellow:

THE CHILDREN'S HOUR

Between the dark and the daylight,
        When the night is beginning to lower,
Comes a pause in the day's occupations,
        That is known as the Children's Hour.

I hear in the chamber above me
        The patter of little feet,
The sound of a door that is opened,
        And voices soft and sweet.

From my study I see in the lamplight,
        Descending the broad hall stair,
Grave Alice, and laughing Allegra,
        And Edith with golden hair.

A whisper, and then a silence:
        Yet I know by their merry eyes
They are plotting and planning together
        To take me by surprise.

A sudden rush from the stairway,
        A sudden raid from the hall!
By three doors left unguarded
        They enter my castle wall!

They climb up into my turret
        O'er the arms and back of my chair;
If I try to escape, they surround me;
        They seem to be everywhere.

They almost devour me with kisses,
        Their arms about me entwine,
Till I think of the Bishop of Bingen
        In his Mouse-Tower on the Rhine!

Do you think, O blue-eyed banditti,
        Because you have scaled the wall,
Such an old mustache as I am
        Is not a match for you all!

I have you fast in my fortress,
        And will not let you depart,
But put you down into the dungeon
        In the round-tower of my heart.

And there will I keep you forever,
        Yes, forever and a day,
Till the walls shall crumble to ruin,
        And moulder in dust away!

There has been a bit of a resurgence of interest in Longfellow or at least in reconsidering him, and this poem is a good example of his unexpected skill. Mostly, though, I want to look at the way he gets at our topic of doubleness, those pesky present opposites. From the very beginning of the poem (and thus as well in its title) Longfellow sets the reader, and the people in the poem, up in a liminal space, the time "between the dark and the daylight," a time which privileges neither day nor night, but which has its own qualities (my son poised at the arrowwood bush, between creativity and knowledge, Keats stuck in his letter between his mind and the world). Then from above he hears the "little feet" of the children. So the parent figure here is positioned as being below the children, in a lower, less exalted place with his, we presume, big clodding feet tucked under a ponderous chair. And which of us hasn't been here in this position? We know they are coming to get us, to ask us for something, to make an observation, to say goodnight, to show us something. We wait like someone stuck in thick mud, nervously expecting some kind of truth. And whether it be a truth of need or desire or imagination, the kids always have something to say.

One can of course hear angels in those "little feet" coming down from above, and Longfellow isn't one to shy away from pat Christian imagery. In fact, angels might be important in a way as bringers of truth here, and in the next stanza we do get a dim perception of that truth. The father sits with a lamp between, we presume, himself and the approaching girls, so he can make them out, but they are obscured in a way, or haloed by the suddenly present lamp light. There also seems to be a touch of Plato's allegory of the cave in this stanza, though it is distorted a bit. The girls, coming as they are from above, from outside the cave, would represent Plato's ultimate truth—the sun; here, unlike in the *Republic*, coming down into the cave. The lamp, then, is the fire in the cave, and the parent figure, our hapless poet-father, is left to be the object casting false images and shadows on the wall. So who is chained up watching the shadow-play? That would have to be us, the readers, though the father in the poem too seems immobile in his chair, both image-maker and watcher—father and false shadow all at once. However, we are given, unlike the chained viewers in Plato, the opportunity to see the truth behind the fire. So sun and angels, cave and shadow, the father and the reader are positioned squarely between two truths, and can see them both.

As the poem continues, the implied cave is replaced by a castled fortress, which the girls easily invade. Interestingly they come in by "three doors left unguarded," so each child has her own doorway into the father's hold. Once again, the father is positioned between, between the three doors, as his cheery assailants rush in on him, and you can do what you want with the imagery of three (fates, trinity, etc.). Either way, in the poem now, the confusion of the lamplight, cave and shadows are replaced by the girls themselves, and the "truth" of what has descended from above becomes immediately apparent. At this point in the poem the girls disappear, they are turned by etymological metaphor into plants in the line where their "arms about [the father] entwine" (like the sinuous wood of the arrowwood perhaps) and the father is left alone, with the revelation of his children.

And here the poem turns truly dark. The father decides that he will, instead of letting the girls go, imprison them in the "round-tower of [his] heart" where they will crumble along with him when he dies. Now, of course, in practice this is just a father attempting to cherish a memory, but it is also a reminder that no memory is sufficient replacement of the present. Now that we know the poet's, the parent's, heart is a dungeon, we can go back to the beginning of the poem and remember that the children are positioned *above* the father, and the father's heart, the dungeon, is positioned *below* the father (as dungeons always are). So not only is the children's hour a time positioned between two kinds of truth (day and night), but the parent is also positioned between two truths—the truth of his children and the truth of his own heart and his knowledge of it. So Longfellow, in the end, does not have a solution for us (in fact, his solution is to grab the things he loves and try to take them down into the grave), but he has made a crucial observation about the state of things—and knowing this, he can turn to his actual children, not just the ones on the page and in the poem, and be more aware. And the reader of the poem can do that too. [1]

Longfellow can *see*, as the poet, the poles that he is split between, but as a parent those poles are much harder to keep seeing, and hard too to pass along that vision. One night I carried our youngest child (just turned three at the time) on my back up the stairs to bed. She of course thought it was wonderful fun, but the minute the older two, who were five and seven, saw me do it, they immediately, of course, wanted me to carry them up too. My gut reaction was to tell them that they were getting too old (or I was getting too old) for me to haul them up the stairs. So they exploded into yelling and half-tears, and I of course relented. As I carried each of them up the stairs we were briefly one body ascending. And, of course, the older one was heavier, so maintaining our unity was more difficult. Though at the time I just thought about my ageing knees and back, later I immediately saw the metaphor. We *can* still come together, parents and children I mean (and we start out that way, in utero, and then skin to skin) but it gets harder and harder and less and less practical. What becomes more the truth is that the natural distance between us becomes more obvious. And I don't think we need always to traverse that distance, but if we know it is there, as Longfellow suggests (the children are on him, but he's thinking of his incarcerating heart), we can feel less bewildered. One day I won't be able to carry them up the stairs, and they'll understand that. But for now, we are between the infant's ease of contact, and that harder distanced place.

---

1. There is lots of other betweenness in this poem too—the fact that the XAXA rhyme scheme gives us always one unrhymed line between two rhymes in each stanza, and also that the metrical character of the poem bounces between the anapest and the iamb so frequently by the middle of the poem that it is hard to say which type of foot dominates the trimeter.

Longfellow has another poem about the distance that time makes:

NATURE

As a fond mother, when the day is o'er,
Leads by the hand her little child to bed,
Half willing, half reluctant to be led,
And leave his broken playthings on the floor,
Still gazing at them through the open door,
Nor wholly reassured and comforted
By promises of others in their stead,
Which, though more splendid, may not please him more;
So Nature deals with us, and takes away
Our playthings one by one, and by the hand
Leads us to rest so gently, that we go
Scarce knowing if we wish to go or stay,
Being too full of sleep to understand
How far the unknown transcends the what we know.

Now, I love this poem for lots of reasons, but, as with "The Children's Hour," I want to focus on how it shows us something about parenting. The poem is obviously, through its extended simile, about death—about "Mother" nature leading us away from the "playthings" of our lives and taking us to the better and higher place of heaven. But what if we do something dangerous here as readers, and read the poem literally? How many times as parents have we enacted this exact scenario, helping our kids clean up their late-day messes—sorting Legos, finding doll heads, disinterring stuffed animals from piles of blocks—and ushering the kids up to bath and bed? It is that journey up the stairs that interests me here. As Longfellow has it, as the child climbs towards bed they are literally between *what they know*, the playtime world of day, and *the unknown*, the mind-led darknesses of sleep and night. On this short journey, the parent is the guide.

Maybe, I find myself thinking, this is our primary role. And don't get me wrong, I'm not saying the parent somehow has more access to the unknown than the child does (quite the opposite perhaps), but we teach and show our children that the journey can and needs to be made—from the world of human knowledge, to the creative world of what is beyond our contexts (like death, like sleep, like dreams, like art). I think Longfellow understood this literal reading of his poem—he was a devoted father, one surprisingly engaged in their rearing for a man who was one of the most public literary and cultural figures of the 19th century. And look how he brings it alive in the poem. Though the mother (parent) is determined, she is not forceful, and by the third line, the child is participating somewhat in the journey, being "half willing, half reluctant" to go. The fourth line suggests the different perspectives of child and parent in its strange description of the "broken playthings." For us, in my literal reading, this is the mess of knocked down blocks and the shoreless sea of unattached Legos. But for the child they are no less for play, and it is up to us (and the mother in the poem) to explain why they must be left behind—traded for the promise of rest and dreams. The child is never wholly convinced, but must, of course, go along.

Then Longfellow does a wonderful thing and shifts perspective. As the metaphor turns, we see the interaction from the child's perspective, and we become (again) a child. Where "The Children's Hour" gives the reader multi-optical vision, "Nature" gives us two perspectives at once (negative capability again) and asks us not to make sense of it, but just to see. The poem is a bit like a mirror—what we've just done to the child is then done to us, we are led "so gently" that we are pleasantly confused, as if the confusion almost were the goal. We are too "sleepy" (so between the states of wakefulness and sleep) to "understand" the difference between the unknown and the known. So this ideal parent has deposited us securely in the liminal space where two things are and can stay true. And it's interesting to me too that, though a religious man, Longfellow doesn't, on the surface at least, turn to religion in either of these poems. It would be too easy, perhaps, to have religion explain the blurring of these borders, and, of course, it wouldn't make sense to the child. We have to see, Longfellow seems to be saying, the "unknown" *outside* of the context of everything we know, including religion. The mystical tradition and all its specific and various theologies of silence and darkness and unknowingness can come later in the parenting game, but with young kids, it needs to stay plain creative mystery.

• • •

One afternoon, when my daughter Lois was still three, I yelled at her, I mean really yelled, and I won't lie, it terrified her. I had been having a morning of frustrations—a forgotten can of evaporated milk spilled out across the fridge, a small shelf was knocked out of the wall, the fire in the woodstove was stubbornly resisting the too-wet hickory I had put in on the coals. I heard from the Big Room a yell of horror from the other two kids that Lois had torn pages from a brand new book. I stormed in and took them from her and told her she couldn't do that, and she, being three, screamed at me and said she could (which from a technical perspective, was correct. . . .).

I roared at her like an engine, "Don't you scream at me!"

Her face sort of melted in fear and she, of course, erupted in tears. I, being too proud in the moment to admit my mistake or the not-so-funny irony of the way I'd said what I said, grabbed her and dragged her to her room. Now, why do we do this sort of thing? It is certainly a momentary loss of perspective, which is possible even when we've learned, from poems or spouses or wherever, that we need to open up and multiply our perspectives. So in that moment, I was most certainly not between any poles—in my lack of wisdom I had retreated just to the self. And isn't this the lesson we strive *not* to teach our kids? It's not the anger that is the problem, or even always the yelling, but it is the pure retreat to the self that damages their understanding of perspective. And the yelling certainly doesn't help. I might as well have just yelled "Me, Me, Me, Me!"—which is basically what she had done.

With this in mind, I'd like to look at one more poem by Longfellow—and it's not one of the many many others of his poems, some very good, some as bad as aspartame, that address children specifically. No, it is the last sonnet in a sequence about a cathedral in Rome, where in his thinking on the complexities of faith, he hits on our innate ability not to understand what we have tried to make ourselves understand:

FROM **DIVINA COMMEDIA**

VI.

O star of morning and of liberty!
O bringer of the light, whose splendor shines
Above the darkness of the Apennines,
Forerunner of the day that is to be!

The voices of the city and the sea,
The voices of the mountains and the pines,
Repeat thy song, till the familiar lines
Are footpaths for the thought of Italy!
Thy fame is blown abroad from all the heights,
Through all the nations, and a sound is heard,
As of a mighty wind, and men devout,
Strangers of Rome, and the new proselytes,
In their own language hear thy wondrous word,
And many are amazed and many doubt.

Though Longfellow is not considered a "great" poet, that last line is great. It is so unexpected at the end of this poem about wonder and understanding and light and more light, and not the least because its rhyming partner is the word "devout." What I love most about the line is that it doesn't draw an obvious syntactic division between those who are amazed and those who doubt; they aren't necessarily different groups of people. Longfellow leaves the door open to the possibility that those who are amazed might also be the ones who doubt. Though this is a poem about faith, we can read it in the context of the other "advice" about parenting we've uncovered in Longfellow, and see that though the parent is meant to be the guide between poles—the known and the unknown, the dark and the daylight, shared human knowledge and individual creativity, self and others, context and contextlessness—sometimes we forget that that is our job, or we forget to do it, or we flat out refuse.

Though he gives us that out at the end of the poem, let's look at the rest of the sonnet to see him set it up with a now familiar trope. The poem opens with the same seesaw between dark and light that we started this whole discussion with, where the "splendor shines / Above the darkness." In this image our world, the human world, *is* that in-between place we've been navigating. The poem continues with a short catalogue of poles—city and sea, mountains and forest. And these aren't necessarily opposites, but certainly different worlds. Now notice that the "song"—which in the poem is faith, but can also be read as poetry, and we could read it as a child—is to become a path, presumably between those worlds. So can we read this as the parent hopeful that one day the child will be just such a path? Certainly Longfellow didn't have parenting in mind in this particular poem, but it reflects his interest in the possibility of made ways—that traversing, or attempting to traverse impossibly separated worlds is the task of the human being, and certainly one of the most important things we can explain, or wordlessly show in the pantomime of our better days, to our children.

Both the second and third poems I've discussed here are sonnets, and Longfellow turned to sonnets more and more in the later part of his writing life (though he wrote them all along to be sure). Thanks to Petrarch, Shakespeare, Wyatt, Donne and others, love is an inescapable component of any sonnet. It lurks in the background the way something primal sneaks into any tune played on a banjo, or the way some pungent root fried in fat begins half the recipes in the world. Love, of course, is the primal component too of parenting, but it is important for us to remember, as Longfellow shows us, that we can't really understand it. *It* is the unknown and the known and the path between. So, as we read Longfellow's parental anecdote in "The Children's Hour," his metaphorical and universal bedtime scene in "Nature," and the final and finally ambiguous poem about understanding faith we've just looked at, we can see love (or Love, or what have you) glimmering through the cracks. And we can see it in ourselves too. There was love inside my screaming at little Lois that morning, and there was love when I gently held the arrowwood fruit and marveled with Rache, and love when we read and think about these poems.

So poems and parenting? Well, they're both about as old as humankind, both perhaps a craft (in the way that crafts require learning and relearning in the forge of experience). Also, Longfellow reminds us that poems try hard to speak to the things that are impossible to say—to find the truths between the truths, as Keats was suggesting. Meanwhile, the final unreachable goal of parenting might be to give your child all the knowledge she needs and wants, without clouding her native sense of discovery and generative delight. But because the perfect poem will never be written, we look to poems also as markers or examples of process; poets and poems can *show* their readers how these in-between truths are sought, and we can learn from them how sometimes we are them. Similarly there are no perfect parents, but perhaps our children can take from us what we might take from a poem, seeing the process of navigating a world of multiple truths, of contradictory impulses, of light and dark. I think the sooner they understand this difficulty, the sooner they will be amazed at who they can be. And, of course, like their parents before them, beautifully, the sooner they will doubt they can manage it.

My Heart in Every Darkness

Watching George Scarbrough Wait
(2015)

Have you ever been around guinea fowl? If not, you can trust me that they are in an elite group of creatures that are consistently louder than small children. Now that might be hard to believe if you happen to be near your kids as you begin reading this essay, but if you happen, instead, to be near a window with a small flock of guineas outside it, you won't be in the least bit surprised. In fact, you probably won't be able to pay attention to this next sentence for very long. Now we don't keep guineas, but there are folks who love them—for their meat and eggs (when they can find them), for their capacious appetite for ticks, and just for their funny way of being in the world. They run everywhere, they scream almost non-stop when they are in the mood, and if they haven't been well-trained from the beginning, they like to run away from home, or at least from our concept of home.

Some neighbors of ours, about a half-mile across a field, sporadically keep guineas, and one spring they had a particularly feisty group of about four or five hens who ran off and decided to set up shop at our house. It's hard to describe the sound of their call if you don't know it, but if I had to try I'd say it sounds something like a Canada goose attacking a car alarm, endlessly. For about two days the guineas stayed around our house, they sent our chickens into utter disarray (chickens and guineas sometimes don't like to have much to do with one another), and we simply couldn't chase them off. They would leave for a few hours and then sure as a tide come squawking back through the woods on their way, I guess, to the especially succulent ticks and grubs in our yard. By the morning of the third day, my wife was ready to make guinea stew, or hats for everyone, or something along those lines.

When I got back from work that afternoon, the guineas were again patrolling the yard, and I decided I had to get rid of them once and for all. I got out of the car, still in my nicer clothes, and began chasing wildly after them. Now if you've ever tried to chase a bird on the run, you know that you, two-footed poorly-balanced bumbler that you are, stand little chance. So I know I made quite the picture for everyone now gathered on the porch watching as I ran from bird to bird getting no closer than a few feet from any one of them. My daughter Jane Bell came down the porch stairs, she was quite young at the time, and she toddled toward one errant bird saying, "Gimmees best friend!, gimmees best friend!," which was funny enough to make me stop running and also arresting enough to make me stop and think about what it must have looked like to her to see me frightening the crazy birds.

Fortunately for our collective sanity, my son Rache, at the time about four, almost at that same moment flung open the porch gate and leapt down the stairs with a Thor mask half-pulled over his face and a broken plastic sword in one hand. He was coming to the rescue. Of course, he had no better luck than I had had, but he had fortuitously neglected to close the gate behind him, and about ten seconds after he arrived, our two pit-bull mix shelter dogs came off the porch like ballshot from a blunderbuss. They instinctively cut off the birds at every angle, and within seconds the hens had taken to the skies (guineas can fly for real) and roosted in an oak tree about fifty feet above our heads, with the dogs barking wildly beneath them. The guineas stayed in that tree for the rest of the day. Later, they flew off and did not come back.

I'd like to follow this story with a poem. Now the poem doesn't have guineas in it, which is too bad, but it does have a vibrant world like the one my kids surely saw me running through that afternoon. The poem is by the too-little-known east Tennessee poet George Scarbrough, from his 1949 book *Tellico Blue*, and is one of the most beautiful poems I know:

EVENING

Awhile at most
And I shall be following quietness
Into these hills, walking up these valleys
Under beloved leprous trees

Where locusts plague the heart and blue
Water sounds over the eerie crying.
Eternally dismissed, I shall become only
A name under the known cover of this earth
Of blue mountains and unintelligible rivers.

This stark beautiful land requires no record,
Is separately indexed under the stones
Slouching brilliantly on the Eastanalle hills,
Looming grayly in the sunless evening on
The spur of hills that grow anonymous when
The red leaves rule the valley
And first and last are confluent into one,
New knowledge covered with an ancient fact,
So time is lost with every generation
And Reuben sleeps as soundly as his sire.

Too much of me is now in every place
Among these uplands where the dazzling stones
Lean in the red and yellow shadow,
And more prepares to die tomorrow and the day after.
For in these hills are lost
The faces counted friend and beautiful:
Like foxes invisible to the day,
They rise and run my heart in every darkness,
Between the rivers of the county world.

Considering these, loneliness is tossed
Upon me like a bouquet out of the evening,
Lostness is like a flower rooted in the orange-red
Sundown, a flower I cannot deal with
In usual ways and pin it with my compliments
Upon the shoulder of a friend.

Well, where to start? At first blush the poem doesn't seem to have much to say to my little story about kids and guineas—the birds with all their squonking wildness and the poem with its almost unutterable sense of quiet—but we'll get there. Let's first look at what Scarbrough is doing in this poem. This is a poem about identity, our sense and senses of self, our relationship to the place around us, to the other living creatures around us, and, finally, to the other human beings around us. Scarbrough does not fall into the trap of easy solitude. Evening, here, does not represent a calm prayerful moment of innervision (to borrow a phrase from Stevie Wonder), but instead a quietness which has both that vision and terror in it—Frost's terror, the terror of being alone in a place. But almost instantly in the poem, this terror (which is more suggested than stated outright at first) is ameliorated not by the inner resources of the poet's soul, but by the comforting and familiar presence of place. The speaker walks among trees which are "leprous" but still "beloved."

This familiarity, however, is not always returned in kind. Scarbrough tells us that the land "requires no record" from man, can take care of itself in other words, that it quickly can "grow anonymous" as the seasons change its face, and time itself can become "lost." This passage has always struck me in two ways—the first way in the way it is intended on the surface. Scarbrough is one of our great thinkers on place; he lived in the same landscape for almost his whole life, and like Berry in Kentucky, Kumin in Vermont or like Lyle in James Galvin's classic book *The Meadow*, it almost let him in. Scarbrough was one of seven children in a sharecropping family, so he knew a lot about community and relationships. He was also gay in a time and place that would not permit him to live with his heart, mind and body fully open to the people around him. So, it is safe to say, he knew loneliness. Though Scarbrough never had children, his experience *as* a child deeply informs almost all of his work, and I can read this poem also through the ears of a parent listening to a child. Like the land, our children can grow anonymous, can seem like they are keeping their own quiet (and not so quiet) records, and that they themselves are the "new knowledge" covering and changing our own conceptions and preconceptions of the world.

With this unusual double reading, let's move on to the third stanza:

Too much of me is now in every place
Among these uplands where the dazzling stones
Lean in the red and yellow shadow,
And more prepares to die tomorrow and the day after.

We're still not to the guineas yet (stay with me), but this is powerful stuff. Scarbrough's bold opening line in this stanza seems to refute some of the glad-handing of a lot of contemporary writing about place (which admittedly comes out of a well-intentioned gloss of Thoreau and Emerson), and, I think, could also refute some contemporary writing about parenting. It's not all juice boxes and play-silks out there. Sometimes we are terrified we have done too much, have shown our kids the wrong sights, have not taught them where to find the dazzling world, have not prepared them adequately for the hard facts of decline and death by filling them with the wrong things. For just as any relationship with the land is bound to be one of loss, any relationship with a child is one that will have death and loss built into its joy. The chickens you keep will die. Your wonderful dogs will die. The forest you love that your neighbor owns will probably be logged. Grandparents will one day disappear. And these losses feel like the world slipping away, the safe world you've tried to show your children. Scarbrough, as a child (and he was still a young man when he wrote this early poem), felt such a sense of loss directly—his cousin Reuben, with whom he was intimately close, died young, and his family moved from place to place, leaving and losing all the while, throughout his childhood. Our children, in their own gradations of understanding, feel these inexorable losses too.

And what we've lost, it feels, is what we most have loved:

For in these hills are lost
The faces counted friend and beautiful:
Like foxes invisible to the day,
They rise and run my heart in every darkness,
Between the rivers of the county world.

But here, even in this darkest of moments in the poem, Scarbrough gives the reader some hope. The lost friends are like *living* foxes—alive, but impossible to see. So these things and people who have left us are still powerfully there, and they "rise and run" our hearts despite themselves. And then that final line of the stanza—that wonderful moment of demarcation of place, where the human world and the natural world merge in the bounding of the self. Neil Evernden in a well-known essay on place, suggests that, like some other animals, we could consider our

"self" to extend beyond the borders of the skin and out to the borders of
our known home places. Here, Scarbrough says the same—the human
world (the county world) is small and known but joins with the wild
world bound too by rivers, and not just lines on a map. And that this is
world enough. It is both a microcosm of the whole world and the whole
world in itself. It contains our joy and our losses, beauty and terror. As I
said before, Scarbrough had no children, but this understanding of the
world is one that the parent must pass along. Scarbrough intuited this
as a child who grew through it, and we can learn as parents from him
here. The guineas understood that their world included mine. I did not
understand that. The dogs, in the instant recognition of instinct, understood. Jane Bell, wobbling out towards them with her hands outstretched
in greeting, also understood.

It seems significant, here, that the poem doesn't end in this darkness.
It turns instead toward light in its shorter coda-like final stanza, and it
turns also toward the incredible power of human connection and community, no matter how small (here just a community of two):

Considering these, loneliness is tossed
Upon me like a bouquet out of the evening,
Lostness is like a flower rooted in the orange-red
Sundown, a flower I cannot deal with
In usual ways and pin it with my compliments
Upon the shoulder of a friend.

Who could have imagined this poised, celebratory, almost black-tie ending to this poem? Who could ever have imagined the word "bouquet" in
here? Scarbrough literally takes the dying sun from the ever-distancing
natural world he loves and pins it into the human world where he also
finds consolation. Every time I read this poem I am struck by the marvelous shifts in diction—both in that visit to the metaphorical florist in the
second line and also in the marvelous description of the sundown as a
flower he "cannot deal with / In usual ways." This move to the unspecific,
generalized language of "deal with" or "usual ways" is the refusal of the
poet to speak—he instead recognizes that what he has to say about "lostness" and about death is impossible to say, so it has to be said in the language of avoidance, the language people (and poets) sometimes have to

use. Or maybe poetry is, in its own way, always a language of avoidance. Maybe parenting is too.

What was I chasing that day when I ran around in the muddy spring garden in my good clothes and my half-good shoes? Well I was chasing something that had to be gotten rid of in some way, but I was also chasing something that couldn't be gotten rid of. In the strange quadrangulation of the guineas, me, the dogs and Jane Bell, we all made one shape—four points connected by spidery lines. In "Evening," Scarbrough understands this relatedness of things—the dying trees are both beautifully and horrifyingly connected to him. The dead, in some terrible yet still lovely way, are not completely dead (the fox is always out there somewhere). And at the end of the poem, Scarbrough sees these connections, and refuses to try to make sense of them, and somehow that is the right move. I think Jane Bell was the closest of all of us to that stance. The dogs followed their instinct to hunt; I followed my instinct to try to isolate my human world from the rest of the world, the guineas followed whatever crazy honking instinct they were following, but Jane Bell saw the world for what it is—completely baffling, but still worth enfolding in the arms of friendship. Now none of this is meant to suggest that we should have invited the guineas in for tea; I'm glad the dogs scared them off. But the situation held a lesson—our kids can see the world in ways that we have trouble sometimes seeing. Instead of seeing the mystery and pushing back, trying to order and rearrange, they see the mystery and simply look past it, set it aside like a knick-knack on a shelf strangely to beautify and be a new part of their expanding world.

Here's another Scarbrough poem that gets at this sort of world-making in another, perhaps more direct and temporal way:

THE SOURCE IS ANYWHERE

The others have gone searching,
Screaming for their find
With one mind.
But I wait here for a miracle
Beside the brook, a revelation
Of time and space they do not know
Who must go

And have gone searching,
Running, walking into the uplands
Carrying in their hands
Discoveries that grow old from one to the next one.
They do not know they meet the head of the brook
With each look,
Each step in their progress,
As last becomes first, the foot
The head, the finder loser.
When they arrive wherever they are pleased
To name the source,
They will but drink
From the end in the beginning.
But I am a lover of the whole course,
And I am free.
I wait at any point along the brink
For what they seek to come to me.

I love to talk about this poem with my students. Scarbrough, who is a master of formal verse (the majority of his work is written with meter and rhyme), uses free-verse here in a very specific way. When we get to that key moment three lines from the end—"And I am free,"—we feel both the philosophical weight and the formal weight of the statement.[1] But, of course, what is really notable in the poem is its Emersonian rewrite of how we look for meaning in our lives. There is a lot of talk in our contemporary culture about "finding" oneself, or "seeking" a more meaningful life, etc. Scarbrough, all those years ago, is challenging that idea of having to search these things out—he is arguing instead that we are all of us already positioned on the banks of life's waters, and all we have to do is kneel down and drink. It is more an act of recontextualizing than of seeking. Kids get this intuitively. We forget it as we get older, we get lost in our concept of the self as a narrative—something with a clear beginning, and more perniciously, a clear end. But the self, if it is a narrative, is a fractured one, one with many starts and stops, many side-plots, many forgotten episodes.

---

1. It is worth noting, however, that despite the free verse, the poem has a heavily iambic character.

Let's look at this poem from the beginning and see if we can make sense of it. Scarbrough infuses the poem with the familiar dichotomies of solitude—the "self" and "others"—in that first line. However, it is not a pure solitude, because the reader seems clearly invited to join the speaker. Then the language becomes nearly baptismal—"miracle," "revelation," "brook," all comingle to create an everyday world on the brink of magic. It is important that within that language of magic, the verb used to distinguish the speaker from the other "seekers" in the poem is the word "wait." While the poet here patiently sits beside the brook, those seekers are "running, walking into the uplands" carrying with them all the baggage of what they have "discovered" before. So, in essence, though the seekers are travelling and searching, their eyes are clouded by what they have already seen. The person waiting patiently, on the other hand, remains clear-eyed and open. This, to me, has enormous resonance for parents—how often have we decided something about one of our children based on something we had previously discovered? How often do we have the obvious revelation that every child is very different from every other child? We are often tempted, as caregivers, as bringers of safety and love, to solve perceived problems, or to solve problems even before they begin. But Scarbrough here is reminding us that just waiting and watching may be the most powerful thing we can do.

I recently took all three of my kids to the optometrist here in town. My wife and I both have rotten vision so we are operating under the assumption that one day all of our kids will need glasses or contacts or what have you. However, Dr. Kingsley told me after Rache had his appointment (while I tensely stood behind him listening to him try to read out the increasingly tiny letters on the screen), that though Rache was clearly near-sighted, he would not recommend glasses just yet. Apparently, he explained to me while I tried to appease Lois, who was on the floor pretending to be a dog, recent longitudinal studies have shown that even for kids that *need* vision correction, the earlier they began wearing glasses, the worse their vision as adults was likely to be. The eyes quit trying to see things properly, he explained, and adapt to the glasses, instead of to the world they are trying to see. So, the sooner you ask their bodies to be different, the less like themselves they will end up being, I guess. (It is worth noting here that they also tried this study on chickens and found the same results, so we get to fill this paragraph with the truly marvelous image of chickens wearing glasses.) As I drove home from those appointments, I found myself, strangely, thinking about Scarbrough's poem. It doesn't hurt that vision is such a powerful metaphor in general, but Scarbrough is certainly talking about the same thing Dr. Kingsley was talking about—work with what you have while you can, find beauty with what you've been given, and, though you may lose it, you'll be stronger in the end.

To flip our focus (like the lens-windows in the optometrist's bizarre prescription contraption) back to the parent in the poem, let's look at what Scarbrough says about origins and endings. He writes in the middle of the poem:

They do not know they meet the head of the brook
With each look,

and later

When they arrive wherever they are pleased
To name the source,
They will but drink
From the end in the beginning.

Earlier I suggested that we might read our children as the brook in the poem. So to continue that reading, then, somewhere in our children, even at their younger ages, are their future selves, who they will "become," and who they have been, *and* who they are. Of course this is true for us parents as well. Who hasn't woken up in the morning or looked in the mirror with the strange sensation that you can't quite remember the last ten years passing? We often sort of forget how old we are. All the time I'll be ordering coffee somewhere or checking out at the grocery store and will find myself bantering with the person working there, tacitly under the assumption that we are both "young" and therefore have something in common. Only later will it hit me that I must look old to those young people, that I am probably twenty years older (or more) than many of them. So were they talking to me or a past self? Is there a difference? And so with our kids, we are still comforting and responding to that beautiful infuriating infant we coddled for months and months, and we are also already talking to the teenager who will surprise us with their thoughtful gestures and madden us with their wills.

If we follow Scarbrough on the journey of his poem, then, we can see our kids as far more complex creatures than they may appear to be at first blush. We can squat down in front of them, like Scarbrough beside his brook, and be both at their source and their final destination, wherever and whatever that might be. And we can love that interaction and intersection, that communion, in a fuller way—

But I am a lover of the whole course
And I am free.
I wait at any point along the brink
For what they seek to come to me.

So I guess we too can be freed from the bounds and bonds of the moment, if we are lucky enough to grasp it. Now none of this is to suggest that we all can become perfectly balanced parents out of some PBS cartoon who never make mistakes, sing songs about anger, and spend all their time planning and guiding their children's emotional and day-to-day activities. But it is to suggest that if we keep Scarbrough's dictum in mind, whether in the moment or in reflection, we might understand ourselves and our kids a bit better. I don't always have to chase them down, I can, in ways, wait for them, all of their selves, to come to me. And then I might actually see them.

So when Rache charged down those stairs in his Thor costume and Jane Bell chased after the guineas with arms outstretched, they were of course living in their moment. But they were also living in the brook-run of the world—the relentless time of "Evening" coursing around them— forming in that moment some kernels of their future lives and also recapitulating gestures and feelings from their past. And in the wild flow of that world around her, why shouldn't Jane Bell have thought those crazy squonking birds could be her friends? Who knew the world could make that sound, and isn't it amazing? The world is full to its creekbank of mystery, loneliness and friends. When you stop and think about the mind of a young child—what could be more alone? While we often think about their magical journeys of discovering all the new things in the world, they are also, like us, profoundly alone. Scarbrough's poems seem to recognize this aloneness in different ways. In "Evening" he tells us that the world is frightening and ours, even a component of ourselves, but we don't have to always explain our fears, that we can take its strangeness for beauty and find friendship in it. In "The Source is Anywhere," he reminds us that in the self, and in the world, are all their previous and past manifestations. To learn about ourselves, we can sit quietly and wait. To learn about our children, we can sit by them and look at them and listen and wait. The sun will set on their cold rushing waters, and it will be beautiful. If we can love the moment, and the whole course, love our children and all their wild impulses, their lonelinesses and their bonds, we too can be free.

Somebody Loves Us All

Elizabeth Bishop Across a Chasm
(2016)

So I've been thinking about caring. We say we are going to *care* for our children or that we *care* if something happens or that we don't *care* for artichokes. But what do we mean? A simple look back through the word's etymology suggests that its true root is something along the lines of sorrow, but by the 16th century it began accreting other meanings—to take in one's hand in *care for*, for instance. It also bears a strong eye-relation to the Latin *caritas* or *charity*, though there is no etymological connection there that I know of. But maybe we can think there is: we sorrow, we hold, we try to do good. That seems about all we could ask for as we try to conduct ourselves in the world.

To care for a person or a thing, or to act with care is an act that takes almost constant vigilance. When our children do something that annoys us, we have to be physically aware of our own possible reactions in order to keep from having the wrong one. In this way, care sort of begins to seem again like *charity*—not the word but the virtue, that practiced by, say, Benedictine monks who spend a lifetime attempting to learn to react spontaneously with charity towards the world. *Care* not just as a taking in hand, but a taking in hand and then giving back. We examine the world then give it back to itself undiminished.

For a parent, or better said, someone like me who is always still learning to be a parent, proper *care* seems almost an impossible goal. We strive, yes, to care for our children every day, but we must also model caring in the world. Who else will? When the kids are rapt and joyous talking to the mouse caught in the live-trap you set out, what else can you do but gather everyone, put on shoes and coats, and hike out down the driveway to release her in the meadow? When you are maybe cheated at the mechanic, you do not yell; you remember that the people who work there, too, are people, and you treat them, with your children watching, with a kindness that has to be remembered—which is practiced, and again, in and of itself, is practice.

There is one poet, for me, who embodies this practice of careful movement, of thoughtful decision-making and patience in the world more than any other, and that is Elizabeth Bishop. Bishop's poems are in some ways indescribably slow—moving down the page like beautiful fish finding their way in barely-perceptible currents, each movement purposeful and varied. Bishop is maybe the only American poet who is both one of our great masters of meter and rhyme *and* of free verse. And it may be that for her it wasn't the form that dictated the style, but instead the care behind it. That care, for us readers, us fellow caretakers, becomes also a model of how to see and understand the world. Here's her poem "Sandpiper":

SANDPIPER

The roaring alongside he takes for granted,
and that every so often the world is bound to shake.
He runs, he runs to the south, finical, awkward,
in a state of controlled panic, a student of Blake.

The beach hisses like fat. On his left, a sheet
of interrupting water comes and goes
and glazes over his dark and brittle feet.
He runs, he runs straight through it, watching his toes.

—Watching, rather, the spaces of sand between them,
where (no detail too small) the Atlantic drains
rapidly backwards and downwards. As he runs,
he stares at the dragging grains.

The world is a mist. And then the world is
minute and vast and clear. The tide
is higher or lower. He couldn't tell you which.
His beak is focused; he is preoccupied,

looking for something, something, something.
Poor bird, he is obsessed!
The millions of grains are black, white, tan, and gray,
mixed with quartz grains, rose and amethyst.

There's almost too much to say about the poem, but I'll try. First off, even the chosen figure of the sandpiper shows Bishop's unflagging career-long commitment to using humble animals as emissaries—I'm thinking of moose, moths, armadillos and others. The sandpiper is an overlooked bird as a species, and here one who is literally overlooked because he is so busy looking. Only the poet sees him—not the roaring ocean, not the swelling tidal earth—there's just the careful eye of this observer observing her fellow observer. And see how she does it—the long-legged slightly off pentameter she uses to match the bird's gait, and the marvelous and often understated rhyming that pulls the poem together. The first pairing of "shake" with the funny comparison to William Blake sets the tone of the poem in a particularly Bishopian way—using humor to suggest something bigger about the subject matter (Blake, of course, was a visionary, who also observed the world in a unique way), which will be recast later in the poem.

We see the care in composition immediately at the beginning of the second stanza, in one of the best similes in all of English-language poetry. With her simple and devastating comment that "The beach hisses like fat"—we at once have a jarring reminder of the human world (our kitchens, our fires), a perfectly accurate comparison (a beach with a wide flat sandy shoreline really *does* sound like cooking), an ominous tone shift in "hisses," and the surprising syntactical variation of a very short sentence. That is a lot to pack into five words. She'll mirror this effect at the beginning of the third stanza with a similarly placed short metaphor. Notice too, how "fat" in the simile sets us up for the rhyme sound of "sheet" and "feet" in the first and third lines of the stanza. This is the sort of thing that Bishop can do that few other poets can do. Each word has a function, is carefully placed. It would be pedantic of me to go through the entire poem listing out the impressive valences and tonal resonances of each carefully chosen phrase, but, suffice to say, they are there—in sound, in meter and in meaning.

But before we leave the poem, let's spend a little time thinking about our sandpiper friend. In what ways does Bishop have him representing the kind of *care* I opened this essay with? She jokingly mocks the bird in the last stanza for his "obsessions"—his looking down and into the world at his feet. He doesn't just want to see it, he wants to see the beauty in it. The list of mineral colors at the end of the poem, ending with the quartz that is "rose and amethyst," not only finishes the poem with a miraculous rhyme (set up initially by "the world is a mist" many lines above), but it shows us that the bird is simply looking for beauty. He is stopping (stooping?) to "see" the roses, if you will—one assumes that the color rose there is no accident. Three lines above that moment, Bishop writes he is "looking for something, something, something." If we take away the wryness of the moment and read the line literally, we can learn something of care here—looking for one thing, then another thing, then another thing, is a sign of a willingness to be careful, a willingness to slow down and look. Perhaps "looking" is the significant word there, playfully overshadowed by the repetition of "something."

To make this a practical thing, we can pull it into our lives. When our kids come to us with a problem, instead of hastily responding with whatever comes first to our minds, whatever seems most likely to solve the problem quickly (or maybe accidentally escalate things), what if we took the time to look for Bishop's three things—the three "somethings" her little bird is sure are there? I remember beginning to teach my son to read music. Rache loved blasting notes on the recorder (and peeling paint off the walls of my brain in the process), but he struggled a bit in our lessons putting all the pieces together—where the notes are on the staff, what the note value is telling him to do, all the while listening to the tempo. He also has a tendency to get frustrated when he is not very good at something right away. So, really, I might have been teaching him music, but I was also teaching him how to value care. If he takes the task apart, and looks at each element of it, say note names, he can begin to master one element (one something), then he can turn to note value (two somethings), and later, think about listening (three somethings). It is, however, up to *me* to model this kind of careful approach. So when I am teaching, I also cannot get frustrated; I also have to remain focused on what is lovely in the moment—my child taking small shorebird steps into the world of music. I've been playing instruments for thirty years. He is just beginning. Begin with care, I think, and you'll end there too.

• • •

A few weeks ago, just at the near-end of summer, we had a storm brush by after dinner. It didn't rain, but we could see the rain in the feather-drip of clouds on the southern horizon, raining in town, most likely, but not out here. Low grey clouds nonetheless built up around us like armaments and we went outside to watch them. We often go over to the field road that skirts the edge of our property and divides us from our neighbor's biggest field. We stood on the hard road and as soon as we left the protection of our tree-ringed acres could feel the blast of the wind rising up out of the storm. It was strong enough even to push us around a bit, just enough to be fun. Jane Bell and Lois held out their arms as if to fly, Rache ran up and down the road scouting out a runway. Kate and I just marveled at the shape of the clouds, the grit of the wind in our faces, and the patterns of current and sway endlessly etched in the surface of the field by the moving waves of beans. I'm sure there is a mathematical explanation for the patterns, but I wasn't interested in that; just their sudden forceful breath-blown beauty.

Maybe there's something of the care we're talking about here in the way *we* watch the world. And don't worry, I'm not going to write one of those hectoring self-righteous essays in which I lecture the reader for not being outside as much as me, or not living in as remote or organic a place as me. We don't go outside every night, though maybe we should. But that evening we did, and it was worth it—to see an unexpected beauty in an unexpected place. It was a newness that even the kids registered. For days after that Jane Bell would ask if we could go feel the wind again, and it was hard to explain how it took a certain storm on a certain day. She just liked the beauty of it, and I can't blame her.

Elizabeth Bishop, for the qualities on full display in "Sandpiper," is someone I turn to frequently for such lessons on watching and feeling. She is marvelously adept at finding beauty in the things we overlook, the animals we accidentally ignore, the cold we shut out on instinct, the people we overlook in our hubris. Here's the first stanza of her poem "A Cold Spring":

A cold spring:
the violet was flawed on the lawn.

For two weeks or more the trees hesitated;
the little leaves waited,
carefully indicating their characteristics.
Finally a grave green dust
settled over your big and aimless hills.
One day, in a chill white blast of sunshine,
on the side of one a calf was born.
The mother stopped lowing
and took a long time eating the after-birth,
a wretched flag,
but the calf got up promptly
and seemed inclined to feel gay.

Almost every descriptive element of this stanza emphasizes the negative. The spring is "cold," the violet "flawed," the hillside covered in "grave" dust; even the sunshine is "chill" and "white"—something out of a tomb (or an Emily Dickinson poem) and not our typical image of spring. The details accrete and build to that final one-line image of the cow's placenta and birth-viscera as being "a wretched flag," something that all readers of the poem quietly, or not so quietly, cringe at in wonder. But look how Bishop then turns the tables on our expectations—the next line has the sudden surprise of the conjunction "but" (I don't think many readers are expecting a turn in the logic after this long) and the equally-sudden change in diction—the whimsical calf being "prompt" and "inclined" and most of all feeling the archaic happiness of being "gay." The poem is, in fact, directed at Gerard Manly Hopkins's famous sonnet "Spring," which opens with the infamously treacly line, "Nothing is so beautiful as Spring—," and then explodes in a riot of epiphanic language. Bishop's poem takes this line as its epigraph yet opens with the opposite sort of spring, which then begins to rot in the smokeless decay of her negative imagery. But out of nowhere, like Hopkins's Christ, the stanza is saved by the blithe simplicity, the simple desire to breathe and be, of a newborn calf.

I think for me, too, the image of the calf, through Bishop's careful eye, shows the reader how much the world can care, if we are willing to acknowledge it. We so often look for and only see the negative; we so often focus on the problems we duly face that we can overlook the care the world takes in countering our suppositions, in responding to our assumptions. Our children, fittingly, are much more like that calf, than they are like the observer here who is watching the world for its chilliness, its wretched reminders of all the things that are failing us, and is suddenly, shockingly, surprised by the new innocence of the calf.

And the poem turns here for good, is shocked into full change:

The next day
was much warmer.
Greenish-white dogwood infiltrated the wood,
each petal burned, apparently, by a cigarette-butt;
and the blurred redbud stood
beside it, motionless, but almost more
like movement than any placeable color.
Four deer practiced leaping over your fences.
The infant oak-leaves swung through the sober oak.
Song-sparrows were wound up for the summer,
and in the maple the complementary cardinal
cracked a whip, and the sleeper awoke,
stretching miles of green limbs from the south.
In his cap the lilacs whitened,
then one day they fell like snow.
Now, in the evening,
a new moon comes.
The hills grow softer. Tufts of long grass show
where each cow-flop lies.
The bull-frogs are sounding,
slack strings plucked by heavy thumbs.
Beneath the light, against your white front door,
the smallest moths, like Chinese fans,
flatten themselves, silver and silver-gilt
over pale yellow, orange, or gray.
Now, from the thick grass, the fireflies
begin to rise:
up, then down, then up again:
lit on the ascending flight,
drifting simultaneously to the same height,
—exactly like the bubbles in champagne.

—Later on they rise much higher.
And your shadowy pastures will be able to offer
these particular glowing tributes
every evening now throughout the summer.

The poem has turned exactly as soft as we might have wanted it to be at the beginning, fulfilling now the promise of Hopkins's quoted line. The lone break in the poem (between this section and the one previously quoted) sits like a chasm of awareness in the poem—we see over and through it only because we are the lucky readers of the poem and not, for once, the person watching. And though some of that toughness remains—the dogwood petals burned "by a cigarette-butt"—here we have imagery of real awareness. The spring is actively awakened (one thinks of Thoreau in *Walden*—"I have never met a man who was quite awake") and it rises throughout this section—deer with their practiced leaps, oak-leaves climbing up the sober oak, song-sparrows "wound-up," and finally the fireflies giving themselves to the poem's final image of gleeful ascension.

So the images are as careful as we've come to expect, but there is another little turn in this poem that one almost overlooks—and that is the sparing and quietly jarring use of the possessive pronoun "your." Early in the stanza Bishop writes that the deer are "leaping over your fences" and later that the moths are laying themselves like offerings against "your white front door." What is going on here? Who is the you? Given the specificity of the imagery here we are tempted to think that Bishop has a particular "you" in mind—the friend noted in the dedication almost certainly—but we can also read this as the "you" of the reader. We are fictitiously, or metaphorically, given fences and a white door—artificial boundaries that are being crossed or lovingly acknowledged by the ambassadors of spring. *We*, the reader, are meant not only to see these images as we read the poem but are meant to understand them as part of the world we too exist in. If we are careful enough to notice what's in the world, it offers itself to us. And perhaps that idea of boundary—those fences, those doors—is what is crossed when the calf gets up. Our inner fences begin to come down when we notice, with care, what is actually around us.

Or what is across the chasm from us. It is hard to imagine a bigger shift in a poem than this one (its turn like one in an upside-down sonnet), and for me it is redolent too of the kind of shifts we have to make in the ways we perceive the things, and the people, around us. When our kids approach us—with a problem, a complaint, with a hug or with a present— that chasm approaches us too. I often think about the ways we are fundamentally alone—trapped always inside our own skin, and the biggest part of life is negotiating that fundamental aloneness. Isn't that, perhaps, what's at the heart of any lapsarian philosophy? That before that mischievous apple, before pissing off any number of gods, we were bodies combined: Adam's rib bone inside another, Plato's pre-sundered many-armed lovers. After it, though, after the angering and the prideful vengeance of whatever god you want to ascribe it to, we were left alone inside ourselves, supposedly seeking and seeking that lost connection.

But now in our world so divorced sometimes from the power of myth, we too easily forget we are supposed to be still seeking. Our kids come to us with their hands out, or their heads hung, and we stare down and into the chasm. What if instead we looked across? What if, like Bishop does in the poem, we were able somehow to notice in our children that gamboling calf, that fresh wildness that always arises from the sparking of an individual spirit?

And remember, that spirit is in us too, and we need to find a way to show it to our children. They see the chasm also, and if they only see us looking down and into it, they will mimic our behavior. Care, as I began considering it here, is the tool we can maybe use to look across. If we address each situation as a new situation, as a moment with its own strange details, its own contexts and valences, then we will see the situation differently. When we notice details, we notice that the full picture is different than we had assumed it to be.

As I'm writing this my wife Kate is putting a puzzle together with our youngest daughter Lois, who is still wearing her new polar bear pajamas, though it is past ten o'clock on this Saturday morning. Lois has been pestering Kate to do this puzzle all morning, and her mother, understandably, has been getting frustrated with the incessant repeated request (as the morning has many other components we are all attending to— getting showered and dressed, making breakfast, cleaning the chicken coop, walking and feeding the dogs, etc.). But, of course, when she finally relents, Lois is very very pleased. If we step back and think about the situation, Kate and I can clearly see that Lois, who sees relatively little of her mom during the mornings of the week, just saw an opportunity to be together. So of course, then we respond to the situation differently. And then there's the care needed to *do* the puzzle—looking together, talking about the picture that is slowly clicking into life. It's almost as if the act itself becomes metaphorical for the situation from which it arose. This is often the case. Let that calf stand up when you can.

I have purposely left aside the most obvious of Bishop's poems to address the idea of noticing and caring, and I won't quote the entirety of the poem here. But it is safe to say that her early and justifiably famous poem "Filling Station" is maybe Bishop's most profound comment on what we learn from trying to see the world without our usual careless filters. The poem, of course, concerns a stop at a gas station, which is "oil-soaked, oil-permeated," a family-owned gas-station with "several quick and saucy / and greasy sons" who help their parents in the family work. It opens with a lot of clever and ironically faux-elitist talk of how dirty the place is, but then the poem turns (looks across its own chasm) and ends when the poet starts to notice the unexpected domestic details of the place:

Why the extraneous plant?
Why the taboret?
Why, oh why, the doily?
(Embroidered in daisy stitch
with marguerites, I think,
and heavy with gray crochet.)

Somebody embroidered the doily.
Somebody waters the plant,
or oils it, maybe. Somebody
arranges the rows of cans
so that they softly say:
ESSO—SO—SO—SO
to high-strung automobiles.
Somebody loves us all.

Are any of us surprised that *care* has brought us again around to love? Bishop, even in her darkest moments, knows that this will be the case. When we see the humanity, which we almost by habit ignore, in other people—filthy strangers, dear friends, even children—we almost immediately see love. It's worth noticing too that poetry itself is implicated in this poem—that making, the pointless craft of making that doily, is clearly indicative of loving care, of the care it takes to love. Bishop almost restitches the doily in the poem—using five of these fourteen quoted lines to describe it, its presence and its composition—suggesting that such craft, such detail in brightening (or just living) lives, is in fact one of our chief necessities. To notice, in a way, is also to make. When we look across the chasm of our skins, when we see, we are also making—the creative mind composing, as Emerson might have had it—but what we are really making when we care, says Bishop, is love.

Kate and Lois finished the first puzzle, a strange landscape of fairies and butterflies, and they are now hard at work on a second puzzle, a bizarre and, frankly, creepy rabbit holding a stopwatch. They are talking and laughing at how frightening I find the picture, but it is coming together with love. The October light is softly pruning the dogwood outside our kitchen windows, turning the leaves a bronzy red, which somehow manages even to reflect its red light into the room. We can all, for once, sense what needs to be noticed. Lois finds a piece with the rabbit's eye; Kate finds a piece with the watch's hands. Autumn and its sudden light, ways of seeing and ways of keeping time, puzzles and care. It's all right there for us all the time I suppose. We are covered in oil. We are surrounded by frost-damaged still-beautiful spring. We are sandpipers sprinting comically along our own endless shores. We can see each other, and we can see the world we live in, but, stuck inside the vessels of our bodies, we can forget that ideal of connecting, of merging. It can't be done, but it can be understood. We can fashion ropes to toss across the chasm, and they'll never be long enough, but in the tossing we have to look across. We'll think for a moment we see ourselves standing on the other side, but it is instead someone else looking down or looking back. It is our children, it is our loves, it is a stranger. We call out to them and wave. I could call out to you on the other side of this essay, even. I'd yell "Hello there!" or "Look at that!" or "What did you say?" and, finally, when we're done, "Take care!"

On the Cusp of Devotion

A Squirrel, Doubt and Geoffrey Hill
(2016)

It would have come to life if I had touched it. I know it. Or I knew it.
I passed the squirrel on a run one winter morning. The slow day was
full of light, though my head, up until that moment, had been cloudy.
Rache had an emergency appointment with a specialist that afternoon to
investigate an abnormality his ophthalmologist had uncovered. It came
to nothing, thankfully, but I didn't know that yet as I ran down our long
county road. As I turned one of the many bends, which leads to a final
approach to the biggest hill on my route, I saw the squirrel, dead on the
side of the road but perfectly whole—no sign of injury, no tire-flattened
back ends, no sad bloodied head, no missing tail. Its grey fur shone in the
bugle light of the cold sun, legs neatly arranged, its one visible eye closed
as if not in death but in petition or sleep. I saw all of this in a matter of
seconds as I approached the small body. And as I ran towards it, I had a
sudden, I don't know what to call it, realization? understanding? suppo-
sition? I don't know, but I had a sure clear feeling that if I stopped and put
my hand on the squirrel, it would come back to life. It wasn't a vision or a
visitation. It wasn't a spiritual awakening, just a second of pure belief, of
hope even, which wiped my mind clear of everything else it had been full
of. It was like taking a sip of a perfect tonic, or like somehow becoming,
for a flash, beauty or love.

Of course, I didn't stop running. I won't call it cowardice or worry. It,
I suppose, was just plain human stubbornness. Stubbornness in being
plainly human, or plainness in stubbornly and humanly being, or something along those lines. But though I left the squirrel there, when I got
home, sweating and red-faced from the cold, I was elated. On that dark

morning of concern—what would the specialist say about our son?—I hurried into the bathroom where my wife was showering to tell her about the squirrel. She laughed and told me I was crazy and also asked why I hadn't gone through with it. I said I didn't know, but that somehow it didn't seem to matter, that next time I would touch the animal for sure. The next morning, after a totally unremarkable and routine diagnosis from the specialist, I was running the same route again. It was winter so the squirrel was still there—stiff and perfect and shining again in the pre-dawn blue. And of course I stopped and put my glove gently on the squirrel's body. It felt hard, dense, like peace, and it didn't stir. Maybe I should have removed my glove, but I think more likely it didn't rise up because it was dead, and that day, the day after I had sensed the complex power of life, I wasn't as sure, as I had been before, that it would warm to my hand.

When I tell this story to my friends, I almost always get one of two reactions. One group stares at me in disbelief (I am not known, I think, for uncynical heartwarming stories of possible animal resurrection) and tries to change the subject as quickly as possible. The other group immediately wants to talk more about beliefs and more about life and more about the griefs and almost-griefs they've had, and they are not surprised by how strange this story seems coming out of my mouth. I agree with both groups; I feel at once the pull of both responses. It is easy to say that the second group has their finger on the pulse of what matters here, but who can deny the skepticism or fear or whatever you want to call what animates the first group? Isn't that why I didn't touch the squirrel? If I had touched the animal and it had risen, this would be much more than a small essay about parenting and poetry, but if I had touched the squirrel that first morning and it had lain still and still dead, I would have had a darker story to tell. I, for one, like the kind of doubt that is shot through with brightness. Put the two reactions together, and you have a pretty good, I think, understanding of faith, or of art, or of love.

So what does this have to do with poetry? You were waiting, I imagine, for me to get around to that. But doubt, or whatever it is we are calling my experience with the squirrel, has a lot to do with poetry. Ben Lerner has somewhat recently proposed that poetry never lives up to our expectations of it, but in some ways I think that that thwarting is a necessary concomitant of beauty—and therefore exactly what we should, and probably do, expect. If we ever experienced an ideal form, perfect beauty, I bet we'd wrinkle up our noses or be made uncomfortable, as with the uncanny valley in animation. We expect beauty, like faith or love, to be complex and possibly contradictory, and when it hits *that* mark—like in "To Autumn" by Keats, for instance, or Elizabeth Bishop's "Sandpiper"—it does it with a kind of perfection that we *can* acknowledge. But I'm not going to write about Keats or Bishop here—I want to focus on another poet full both of doubt and whatever comes after it—Geoffrey Hill.

Hill is famously "difficult," and, I suppose, difficultly famous. Most American poets I talk to haven't read him much; for years he didn't even have a publisher in the US, even though he was often referred to as England's greatest living poet (or, the GLP, as one of his old Cambridge colleagues once told me he was known amongst other faculty there). He is also often referred to as a "religious" poet—a sort of epithet almost, often used to diminish a writer's work, to make it somehow genericized or lesser. We don't do this to Donne or Milton or Herbert, so why contemporary writers should be abashed at their subject is a bit beyond me. But all that aside, Hill wrote beautifully about doubt *and* faith, about the natural world *and* the bitter human world, about difficult history *and* the difficult present, in traditional forms *and* in new forms. These things were always combined for him, mixed up, part of an almost indiscernible whole. Verse is never free, the natural world never divorced from the world, true doubt never without faith.

For years I have carried around in my briefcase (and have read hundreds of times) Hill's small fourth book of poems, *Tenebrae*. This book, a stern meditation on responsibility, doubt and love is at once Hill's most formal and most daring book. It opens with "The Pentecost Castle" a marvelous part-translation of devotional Spanish poems. Here is one small section of that poem which hits precisely on the combinations and contradictions I've been discussing:

And you my spent heart's treasure
my yet unspent desire
measurer past all measure
cold paradox of fire

as seeker so forsaken
consentingly denied

your solitude a token
the sentries at your side

fulfillment to my sorrow
indulgence of your prey
the sparrowhawk the sparrow
the nothing that you say[1]

What can we learn from this? The small poems that make up this sequence are all notably oblique—vaguely addressed to a Christ figure, a savior who stays maddeningly at arm's reach, or even further, perhaps at a shadow's reach. I marvel at the number of paradoxes crammed into this tiny poem: spent treasure, measurer past measure, cold fire, denied consent, fulfilled sorrow, hawk/prey, nothing said. The oppositions pile up to such an extent that they come to have, instead of a negating effect, a combinatory one. I mentioned Keats earlier, and perhaps one might be thinking of his "negative capability" again here, and it is possible Hill has that in mind too—but Keats wasn't, I don't think, thinking of belief or faith there (except perhaps of faith in art). Hill though, like Keats, does want us to know here that believing/doubting is an exercise, like push-ups, that strengthens one's ability to live in the world. This is something we, too, as parents or lovers or friends, can learn from. Let's look at that first line for instance, a "spent heart," though seemingly a negative thing, can also be read as a heart that has done its work—a heart that has been busy loving. And that love, the love given to others, is the best treasure available to us. Notice how the next line suggests this by pitting "desire" against love, as if they might be almost opposite things. The "spent heart" has kept its desire. One can also read that line as a desire for faith, waiting to be spent, but that too is both a sad and beautiful thing; desire, a heat that burns within us, but is cold in the way it treats us, leaving us always wanting. These are the kind of paradoxes at which Hill excels. I both desired and did not desire to touch the squirrel, and in a way did both.

My eyes are also drawn to one of the plainest, and most unusual, lines

---

1. from "The Pentecost Castle," from *Broken Hierarchies* by Geoffrey Hill, ed. Kenneth Haynes, ©2014. Reproduced with the permission of Oxford Publishing Limited through PLSclear

in the poem: "your solitude a token." I have thought hard in my own poems about solitude and what it means to us, and here in this poem about confused faith and sure doubt, I am struck by what it might mean. It seems Hill is alluding to the crucifixion scene at Calvary—Jesus both alone and joined by the two "thieves" (the sentries at his side)—but he is also reminding us of our own constant solitude. It is so pervasive as to be just "a token," a given feature of our lives. We are at once always alone and also always part of a community, and what's more, loved. Alone and loved. That's a good description of being in a family, I'd say. I challenge anyone out there reading this with smallish kids to find a true moment of what we normally think of as "solitude" in his or her house. You are always surrounded by others. But at the same time, no one else can get into your head. It is a conflict of presence and, in a way, it is our fundamental situation. A situational paradox, perhaps, and love is what excuses or bridges the gulf. True solitude, then, not the boring alone kind, is the aftereffect, the hangover of love.

Let's turn now to a darker poem, this one from the sonnet sequence, "Lachrimae," which forms the spiritual or devotional or unsure core, you might say, of Hill's book:

THE MASQUE OF BLACKNESS

Splendour of life so splendidly contained,
brilliance made bearable. It is the east
light's embodiment, fit to be caressed,
the god Amor with his eyes of diamond,

celestial worldliness on which has dawned
intelligence of angels, Midas' feast,
the stony hunger of the dispossessed
locked into Eden by their own demand.

Self-love, the slavish master of this trade,
conquistador of fashion and remark,
models new heavens in his masquerade,

its images intense with starry work,
until he tires and all that he has made
vanishes in the chaos of the dark.[2]

We could begin remarking on this poem by again pointing out the numerous paradoxes Hill is working with. It is a theme of the book and no surprise to find them here. They become, as the book progresses, a hallmark of the kind of faithfulness (or faithful faithlessness) Hill is exploring and questioning. But in this poem he turns to something more related to the specific paradox I finished with above—that of solitude and community. Here Hill writes warningly of solitude's ugly step-brother, "self-love." He sets him up here in this poem as a kind of minor god we too often turn towards. What does this have to do with doubt? I think Hill is suggesting that when we run into the paradox of faith and doubt (or maybe any of those we've run across thus far) we become afraid and turn to self-love for escape. I admire the way he fashions this god as a "maker" (those of us who make art should start to feel a little squirmy at this point), someone who is wonderfully skilled, creating "intense" images, "starry work" which sparkles and beguiles. The "new heavens" are tempting, but not, one realizes by the end of the poem, a real or lasting thing.

The reader does not have to be a believer in any particular religion (and Hill himself was not) to understand the difficulty of trying to keep this minor god at bay. But the true solitude I alluded to earlier, which we might equate with the sort of "true" faith which often eludes Hill's speakers, cannot be involved with the god of self-love. In this poem, Hill is interested in what will last. He believes that what we build through pride and selfishness will vanish like a light show, whereas humility and groundedness and awareness leave permanent traces. That is something to go on. Elsewhere, in an interview, Hill paraphrased a choreographer acquaintance in saying that the goal of art is expressiveness, not self-expression, and that has always resonated with me. I think it speaks, even, to more than just the pursuit of art—doesn't it speak to our role, say,

---

2. from "Lachrimae" from *Broken Hierarchies* by Geoffrey Hill, ed. Kenneth Haynes, ©2014. Reproduced with the permission of Oxford Publishing Limited through PLSclear

as parents, as well? If we think only of ourselves when we interact with our kids, we rarely get very far. Also, it is easy to forget sometimes that our kids are not just mere extensions of us, but are instead their own divine amazing isolated connected perfect imperfect selves. The last line of "The Masque of Blackness" is a bit terrifying to read as a parent, I suppose— that we will, in fact, vanish into the dark right before our children's eyes one day, but, in that sense, I do not think we should be afraid. We should instead aim to keep as much of our love contextual, not focused basely on the self as the poem reminds us, and *show* our kids what that looks like, an active focused love.

We will screw up, though. One weekend I was out with my wife in a coffee shop, and we had Lois, then four years old, with us. Earlier in the week we had, for no real reason other than the ones we create, bought her a small toy as a treat (there are not toy stores in our town, and we happened to be in Richmond near a lovely one). Well, she decided that that meant she could expect more such toys in the ensuing days, and when they were not forthcoming, she got rather upset. In fact, she pitched an all-out crying nearly-hyperventilating fit about wanting another toy. Needless to say, in public, it didn't make us feel too successful as parents. And there was my self-love. I was immediately as aware of how the situation affected me as I was of how it might have been affecting her. It's true, she was loud, which was making it hard to relax or think, but, that, of course was not what I was upset about. I was embarrassed, and oftentimes embarrassment is the worst form of self-love. (Was there even, perhaps, the same kind of embarrassment lurking inside the idea of touching that squirrel? I wonder . . .) If we could teach our kids, in general, to forgo shame, it would be an enormous gift. Now, I don't mean shame as in remorse—those are different things—but shame as in a simplistic negative awareness of the self. It is in giving in to that awareness that we create, I'd say, the bulk of Self-Love's starry masterworks, which for many become stony fortresses that are hard to see out of but all too tempting to defend.

Hill returns to these themes—the aimed-for distrust of the self, the confluence of faith and doubt, the maddening darknesses of believing in goodness—again and again in this book and in other poems. To finish up, I want to turn now to a much less well-known poem—one, in fact, which wasn't published in its entirety until Hill's work was collected in the massive *Broken Hierarchies*, released in 2013. The poem in question, "Hymns to Our Lady of Chartres," was begun in 1982, so just a few years after *Tenebrae* was published, but not finished until 2012. Scholars surely will parse out what exactly of the poem was written and revised when, but I'm not that interested in that. I'm interested in the spirit of the poem, which despite its lengthy period of composition, still seems organic, and one which seems clearly tied into some of the motivations behind the poems we've already discussed. The poem is an apostrophe of sorts to the Virgin Mary. Hill's voice is at once that of the abashed almost-disciple and the wry skeptical student. There are moments, too, where he seems to take stock of his entire career of thinking on matters of belief. Here's section fourteen from the poem:

Impossible to think of you as France.
You could be in Yunnan, probably are;
I sent you out of my mind for a dare
centuries past and have heard nothing since.

What a deciduous nonsense there is
when the climate changes, my evergreen!
It is not you I address, great Chartreine,
nor the abundance of your known mercies;

though I confuse many by writing so
much on the cusp of devotion, so set
in the metrics. And I misinterpret
myself many times as inviting you.

This is a primitive animation.
I am bemused that it works; but work it
does, with sparks breaking out of the circuit—
old tramwires, old dodgems' besplat motion.

In a school lab I severed a live flex,
the shock like a bursting bag, my heart's

pace snagged across the bunsens and retorts:
sparkler-haired scarecrow, idiot-crucifix.[3]

Well, what to say? One immediately notices the chattier tone in this excerpt, as compared to the sonnets and terse stanzas of the poems from *Tenebrae*, a hallmark of his later work. However, Hill is still notably formal—the stately Italian quatrains move down the page with precision, and the poet himself even notes the connection between devotion and form (a connection I find very satisfying—perhaps the ultimate proof that form and content are always tied together). Let's start at the top of the excerpt—Hill's casual address to this holy figure itself is notable—especially when one thinks back to the very rigid and formal tone of "The Masque of Blackness." Hill seems more comfortable addressing this figure, I suppose, or, perhaps, even he is more comfortable now with the paradoxes of thinking about belief. What he most wants to tell us here, I think, is that doubt and faith (or whatever we're calling the subject of this essay) are not things to be trifled with. In the third and fourth lines, he jokily recalls the youthfulness of skepticism, "I sent you out of my mind for a dare / centuries past," but then also shows us the large consequences: "and have heard nothing since." Now let's be clear, Hill is not chiding readers for not being Christian believers or not being any other sort of believer, but instead is showing us the difficulties inherent even in true doubt. There is always a cost.

Next is the beautiful stanza about evergreens and mercy (Hill is fascinated by the concept of mercy) and then the stanza on which much of the entire poem hinges. I'm sure Hill wrote this section in the later period of the poem's composition—the tone of retrospective seems unmistakable, but in it, too, is still some of the awe of the earlier work. Here the great difficult poet is as clear as he could possibly be: "I confuse many by writing so / much on the cusp of devotion." Hill points out that often the "cusp" of devotion looks a lot, to the outside observer, like devotion itself. But not so. The cusp of devotion still leaves room for some of the doubt we were talking about earlier—and in fact "true"

---

3. from "Hymns to Our Lady of Chartres" from *Broken Hierarchies* by Geoffrey Hill, ed. Kenneth Haynes, ©2014. Reproduced with the permission of Oxford Publishing Limited through PLSclear

devotion, might be an impossible state, or a very difficult state to reach, something like enlightenment or peace (or like that perfect poem). But most of us, I think Hill would say, even those who see themselves as real believers, remain poised on the brink of devotion, or better said, standing between devotion and near-devotion. Hill himself admits to confusing the two states. He writes, "I misinterpret / myself many times as inviting you." These two lines powerfully recall, not in word choice but in tone, George Herbert's "Love III" in which the speaker has been invited to sit and eat a meal with a feminine Christ figure. Hill, however, inverts Herbert's sensual poem about giving in to the mystery of belief and pseudo-pompously makes himself the inviter. Of course Hill has his tongue in his cheek here, knowing, as is made clear in other poems and even the rest of this one, that belief or mercy or love, for instance, do not need our invitation or permission.

We'll come back to the next stanza, Hill's last word on this sort of half-belief, but let's jump ahead to the final image for now. As is often true in poems about complicated subjects, an image will do wonders in wordlessly concluding things—a nod to Hill's modernist precursors I suppose, but here the image is so wrapped up in the person of the writer it seems something else also. It is important for the image that this electrocution happens as a youth—the innocence of youth can allow for fantastic complexities of belief. And then the simple observation that true insight, the shock of awareness of the world, is often an accident, something we don't expect. In fact it is frequently the opposite of what we expect. Love is thrown into the bargain with the marvelous line break in "my heart's / pace" in the second line of that stanza, and we see the heart swell and involve the entirety of the school lab (with the incredible double use of the word "retorts"). And what of the lab? That faith is always an experiment? That even in the domain of science—the historical enemy of belief—these shocks can occur and last? What remains, of course, is not the continuation of shock (that sort of sustained awareness would be impossible to bear), but the aftereffects ("the aftermark / Of almost too much love" as Robert Frost put it)—the young, shocked student overwhelmed by his mistake, Herbert sitting at the table, any of us faced finally and beautifully with a world free of Self-Love's edifications. The young Hill stands as a cartoon cliché of Albert Einstein, "sparkler-haired" (so something's still burning), momentarily genius and simultaneously a fool. Is there a difference? Hill suggests, if we are lucky, we will doubt ourselves towards own foolish rood.

And now that final word on the previous stanza. Just before this image, just after Hill discusses his near-devotion, he calls it (the poem itself perhaps) a "primitive animation." He says he is "bemused that it works; but work it / does with sparks breaking out of the circuit." Not only does he set up the final image, but he gives us the most important thing to think about here. Even the simplest bringings to life matter. If I had raised that squirrel from his death, it would have been more than primitive, of course, but what I did do with it, I believe, is what Hill is talking about. In almost believing in the animal's resurrection, I, primitively, crudely, humanly, brought him to life. This may be the best we can do sometimes. And it left its mark on me ("sparkler-haired") or I wouldn't have begun this essay. What seem like the simplest things—believing in old stories, believing in magic, believing in poetry, believing love—are the things, it turns out, we really need to animate our lives. Hill recognizes this simplicity and is "bemused," bemused because it has taken a whole career to recognize it. I imagine his parents could have told him something along these lines. But who can truly expect their children to listen? We can only give them the tools to later be "bemused." Who, really, can advise on matters of doubt or belief? If you think you can, you probably shouldn't. We must be models, of course, but even that is a tall order. We just have to get out there and hope we hit a live wire from time to time, and we have to hope that our kids are there to smell the smoke, to believe, or doubt, that it ever happened.

I Believe in Myself Slowly

The Perfect Imperfections of Primus St. John
(2017)

When you sit down to think about imperfection and where it is manifest in our lives, it's hard to know where to begin. For instance, even as I was writing that first sentence, I was reflecting on what a beautiful summer morning it is here today—the steam from a wet July Fourth night rising off the meadow as I jogged by this morning, the blueberries at the far end of the yard just beginning to stop their blushing and be blue, cantaloupes stretching new-found arms across the garden rows. The kids, all up too late last night—sparklers and watermelon and friends—are slowly making it into the day by watching Netflix in the other room. But they were, moments ago, laughing and singing along to the tinny theme song of whatever show they'd found. Despite the screen-induced guilt that flickers like a pilot light down in my twenty-first century parenting self, it was a happy moment. Then (you knew this was coming) the screaming started. Someone was putting their feet in someone else's face, someone couldn't see over someone else's big head, someone was choosing the wrong show, someone was breathing wrong. The ideal of a moment shattered by the imperfection of a normal day.

So normal, but that imperfection can be immensely frustrating. One thing about perfection is that somehow, despite being daily shown otherwise, we still think we can aim for such an ideal. It's like Charlie Brown and his football (thank you Charles Schulz for filling so many of our childhoods with a big dose of pathos)—Lucy always pulls the ball away. I can remember spending hours in my grandparents' house in Nashville, Tennessee reading the original Peanuts books and feeling so sorry for Charlie Brown. Though now I can see the joy (or something darker but like it) in his still always trying. Despite our awareness of the near-sureness of imperfection, or even failure, we still can always try. Hope, weirdly, is itself a kind of already-realized joy. So when the day dawns as calmly as this one did, some comical but faithfully romantic part of me still thinks it might last, though my kids are often, always, gearing up to prove otherwise. It is up to us, as both recipients and makers of imperfection, to decide what our reaction will be. Will we be frightened of life's limitations? Angry? Will we ruthlessly pursue perfection? All of these seem like valid responses, all with their own rewards and dangers too, I suppose.

A poet who has thought for a career on our limitations, and the world's limitations and imperfections, is the under-valued Primus St. John. St. John is perhaps best known for *Dreamer*, his 1990 book-length medita-tion on slavery and the responsibilities it still calls us to. But that book also, along with his three other slim books, spends a lot of time thinking simply on what it means to be human—what responsibilities *that* calls us to, and the ways we often fail in recognizing our movements through the world, or the world's movements around us. Here's an early poem from St. John's first book:

A POEM TO MY NOTEBOOK, ACROSS WINTER

The flock of birds takes shape.
            If there is faith
In the world, today
It is scattered, and the space
Is lonely,
High up there, and cold.
            The leader
—I am afraid of these birds—
Thumps for things . . .
This is hope or
It is not a poem.
The tradition keeps flapping,
            Wrong,
Across the sun,
Obtrusively like an author's intervention.

It's incomplete, rich experience,
But the best tip yet is dipping,
Then diving, deep to the left...
           I hope

First of all, I love the tongue-in-cheek awareness of the artificiality of artistic revelation built into the first line. We can see just at a glance that the poem itself resembles those flocking birds, but the writer is all too aware that that is as close as he'll get to understanding them. We cast and recast the world in its own image, he seems to say, but that is not the same as really *seeing*. Ours is an imperfect sight. The poem is about keeping faith—perhaps sometimes a religious faith (as St. John suggests in other poems), but also just faith in the world, faith that we can understand and be. It is not an easy faith, either. The birds represent the trust he's looking for (the perfection we seek)—but it's frightening—the space between them is "lonely," and the leader of this bird-movement, this reminder of what we seek, is scary. He makes demands, and the poet doesn't know how exactly to respond.

Just after that moment of admittance, the poem turns with the beautiful lines, "This is hope or / It is not a poem." There is always hope, he seems to say, in attempting to recognize the world. Or even if we feel inadequate to the demands that faith puts on us—even if we turn away ashamed or run away screaming—a poem, like this one, shows us that that faith is still out there, if only barely accessible by us. And look, this poem of total inadequacy, where the speaker feels utterly lost and left out by these cold high birds, has a real revelation built inside it. St. John writes, "It's incomplete, rich experience" just before the final image of hope in the poem. I love that small comment—that experience can be "rich," full of meaning, without feeling complete, or perfect. In those four words, St. John really gets at the idea of imperfection that I've started with here—morning is beautiful and complex, but it is not perfect. Our lives are too complicated even to explain for a minute, but we hope still to complete the picture one day. We have to, St. John seems to suggest, at once recognize the "richness" of what we are experiencing, and the "incompleteness" of our awareness and of our response.

For his part, St. John's response is frequently to keep still and keep watching. In "The Fountain," also from his first book, he writes that when he hears our lives pouring like a fountain he "[believes] in all of the storms—/ where it came from," and then pretends to be a "mossbacked" prophet (so fantasizing about becoming one with the world) who just sits and waits for understanding to come. The poem concludes with the fountain telling him: "We are all pouring toward the same conviction / . . . / But we believe that, separately." St. John's response is to say "So I believe it all—/ The whole thing's that mindless." And maybe this is a less dark iteration of the same thing we see in "Poem to My Notebook . . ." We believe despite the evidence, or because it seems we shouldn't. To be "mindless," he maybe suggests in this short poem, is to have our minds, if only briefly, out of the way, allowing us to be more fully human.

St. John is possibly thinking about meditation here, I'm not entirely sure, but I know I might think of this poem when I'm faced, as I was this morning, with the unavoidable presence of imperfection in our lives. My love for my kids is so big as to be undefinable, but they test it (enlarge it?) every day by being unpredictable, rushing, wild fountains of thought and emotion. I think they and I most certainly are "pouring toward the same conviction"—that complex love will more and more bind us together, but, of course, we believe that separately. We go about it our own ways. I seem to think we need some rules in the house to keep things sane. They are fully against sanity. They succumb to a few of the rules; they convince me to be wilder. What I should do, more often, is see myself as waiting and watching. When Jane Bell wants to do headstands in the den, when Lois wants to paste Band-Aids all over her critically injured stuffed dog, I should relent, and listen to the water rush by. I should watch for the wings in the sky above us to tip my way.

. . .

There's a twenty percent chance of storms today—now later into July and fully into a real dry spell. Sometimes here in Virginia summer seems suddenly to put on the brakes—what was green and exploding with wet and growth all at once stops finding rain. What clouds there are move by unnoticing and cruel. The heat slowly rises each day and the winter squash in the garden droop their sad leaves in the blistering sun. It's as if, some summers, the whole world around me is being lulled, or drugged, into some sort of uncomfortable sleep. All we know is heat and bright, and it becomes more and more difficult to see the world's gradations.

Yesterday my son Horatio insisted, despite the above-ninety temperatures, that we all walk the circuit around our neighbor's farm. There is a field road there which loops around about a mile—it passes a cow pasture and slowly turns downhill towards Horsepen Creek. There, in the lowest patch of land for miles around, the creek winds through some wild pea and poison ivy and sycamores. It is beautiful at all times of year—though too choked up with the poison ivy in high summer to get down to the water, at least for the kids. However, I, on that sun-oven afternoon, resisted going on this walk at all—too hot for the little one, too late in the afternoon, I was feeling lazy, etc. There was nothing to see. But in the end Rache won and was right—at least down by the creek there was a lot to see: old landmarks that had changed in the turn of this year (we hadn't been down there for a few months), the original bridge over the creek really rotting now into ruin, dry flood-made spring-runs alongside the creek deep as small canyons, which the kids leapt like fawns across.

As we turned back west toward home, passing the pond and the healing clear-cut around it, I found myself walking with Lois (our littlest), and we worked together to get up the two big hills the road drapes over there (my wife Kate, done with the heat and my sudden poet-y enjoyment of it, had gotten way ahead of us with the two older kids). Lois puffed and complained a bit, but also noticed the feel of the wind in our face—surprising like something that is always there for you to find. She wanted to know about the corn growing alongside the road, and when I peeled back one of the young husks to show her its little golden pegs, she was delighted and wanted to peel each one (it's not our corn, so I demurred). So up we walked, not sleep-walking through the heat, as is so easy to do, but more and more awake to the way the imperfect world surprises us.

Here's another poem by Primus St. John that touches on this way of handling imperfection:

LYRIC 13

With emotion
The wind holds out its empty hands.
Let's stop all this; let's stop.

The dry grass stands up
In the dust it must learn to live with
And laughs and laughs.

Such tormented lovers
Have at last found trust.
And I wonder this morning

Outside near the edge of everything
Was I really awake when I saw this.

So beautiful this humble little poem. This lyric comes from St. John's second book and is one of many such fragmentary observations scattered around that strangely constructed volume. I love so much about the poem—the voice is a similar one to the first poem I discussed—this observer who feels at once a part of the world around him and also surely separate. But there is a sense in this poem of seeing for the first time—the personified wind is suddenly filled with a recognizable kind of grief or pain. The speaker feels like he can barely believe it. And then the grass "stands up" laughing at the wind's strange, and impossible, request. So who, I want to know, in the third stanza, are the lovers? Is it the grass and the dust, as the syntax of the previous sentence would suggest, or is it the wind and the grass? The man and the world? Or is it the emotions suggested in the first line? Is it pain and laughter, ache and joy that have found trust in one another? St. John, of course, is too good of a poet to decide for us, or for himself, and instead wants to know if he was "awake"—if he had understood things correctly. Or, perhaps, leading my mind back to my little hike around the field, maybe this kind of understanding, on the edge, watching, is what being really, actually, awake might feel like. Perhaps *that* is the distinction St. John is drawing here—the difference between awake and really awake (maybe hearkening back to Thoreau). Maybe when we are really awake, we see and understand the imperfections themselves—the grieving wind, the mocking grass, the death-like dust—as the beauty we were after all along.

• • •

But it is so hard to stay awake to everything. Raising kids in the United States has many pitfalls, and one of the hardest things to make sure your kids are awake to is the reality of race in our culture. As a white person, whose life has been no struggle in the meanest sense, I feel almost completely unqualified to explain to my children the full ramifications of what our culture's insistence on race as a tangible thing does to us. Kids, of course, are more perceptive than most adults give them credit for, and they know that we all have some explaining to do when it comes to race in this country. They can feel the burden of history on them—who can't when they drive through a nearly-segregated small town like the one we live outside of? But kids don't want it explained away. They don't want merely to feel guilt either. They want to be awake to what it is we have done, are doing and can do; they want to see the corn beneath the husk, I suppose.

A few weeks ago, my family went to a political fund-raising brunch at the volunteer firemen's auxiliary hall. We were meeting a friend there who was running late. While we stood outside the hall, we waved to the other people coming to the breakfast, almost all of whom were Black. As these fellow community members entered the hall, I realized that I knew none of them. Even in this little town of ours. I was so disoriented that I went inside to check to make sure we were at the right place. The kids were totally content running around outside and seemed unconcerned. Kate was concerned about our missing friend, but seemed also unimpressed by my confusion. What was it that made me feel suddenly out of place? Our difference in appearance? A sense of estrangement from what I must internally have perceived as my community? I was even hesitant, for days, to sit down and write this particular part of this essay. People, parents, and maybe white parents especially, find it very hard to take stock honestly of the realities of race around us, to the fact that active awareness is required, and to the responsibility we have to try to show our children what that kind of awareness looks like. I'm not saying I have worked off any guilt here, by the way. I'm still fighting my way through the paragraph. No action feels enough. It is instead a wakefulness I need to pass on—us somehow awake to the true heat of the day, awake to the beautiful difficulty of community, to our communities of difficult beauty.

There are a lot of difficult moments in Primus St. John's major poem on slavery and race, "Dreamer," but here my mind returns to a moment partway through the poem where his main character, John Newton (the composer of "Amazing Grace") is beginning to regret his own participation in the slave trade. St. John writes, in a flash of lucid commentary:

The trouble with atonement is it is like
a sphinx, several parts human, several
parts bull, dog, lion, dragon, or bird.
When we are dreaming of atonement, no
matter how subtly, we must remember
we are not dreaming of a verb.

Strong stuff. It is easy quickly to rebuke this by saying that, in fact, actions are important, louder than words, as it is said (all the self-righteous smugness of some protests with witty signs and "Hey, hey, ho, ho" chants comes to mind). But St. John, here, is backing me up I think; no action is enough. What is more important is the noun at the heart of the verb. Atonement is a state, a putting together, *inside oneself*. Actions, he argues here, are external manifestations of what *things* are inside. And what is inside might be an ugly mess. But we have to work towards putting things right in there.

He foreshadows this moment in an earlier passage:

If this is a story
Of the reasoning of slavery,
Where are we?
What have we been doing
To people,
To the light
From which life emanates?

Slavery is a story
Of procreation,
Of magical religious thinking,
Of the androgynous divinity
Within us.
No story can be this happy
Unless it is married
To something deeply within us.
It is not them
Who have done it to us,
Or us

Who have done it to them.
It is the antagonistic dream
Of unreconciled love.

Few writers I know of are as bold as St. John, and the difficult point he is making hides behind the careful line breaks. At first one reads this passage and wonders how the poet could *not* assign blame to the white slave traders (who he excoriates in other parts of the poem). But our easy reading has us miss the point. St. John wants us to look past the verb ("have done") and towards instead the nouns: us and them. He is arguing in the passage that we must not understand the two sides as an *us* and a *them* but instead as just an *us*. We are unrequited with ourselves. The procreation—the erotic, even, desire for love—he hints at in the beginning of this passage is a procreation with ourselves. A making whole and bearing from that. We must, he says, aim for a state of real atonement, but also that merely aiming is not enough. We must try really to know the noun in our sights.

At the end of "Dreamer," St. John keeps thinking of dreams. Writing of Newton (who was an enslaver and then, later, an abolitionist), the poet says:

I dream I will not be forgiving him
for the timeliness of his innocence, for
betrothing the dead to the dead,
but will be lifting
up my hands to an appetite for life
that will take slavers and slaves with me.

So St. John, who sees himself in the poem as a possible vessel of atonement, is also pretty angry. It is important when we talk about love and forgiveness that we keep in mind that such things are not always quiet and sweet; they are in fact rarely weak or submissive. There can be a lot of anger in love, and difficult strength in forgiveness. Notice that in the above passage St. John says at once that he will not be forgiving Newton in the traditional sense, but will instead push upwards through him, will raise his hands in a gesture of union, of bringing together, of atoning. How different our ideas of atonement and forgiveness really are, we realize here. And the poem ends angrily—it wishes that slavery was something far away, something distant and historical, "but it is *right here* / In my pouch, today, / Like the acori beads I have been swimming with / For hours—." So the painful is mixed up with the sacred, carried around with us every day, in our pockets, in our imperfect hearts.

And I guess that is what I was reminded of that day outside the firemen's hall; I forgot, as I so often do, my everyday duty to know what I've got with me—to recognize that the reason I didn't know those people streaming into the same event I was going to was my own inaction, or my own trusting in my own actions. I thought I had done enough to be a part of my community, or I told myself that my actions have been enough. I forgot about the nouns inside: my own quiet racisms, my privilege, my responsibility to love and atone, even my anger. For my kids, I realized I must try harder to bring those things, these imperfections, out into the open more and acknowledge them, to make myself more aware of myself. Again, we are modeling here. Kids are not always introspective creatures, but they can see us and absorb the way we take stock of our own natures.

St. John can step in here again to make me feel better. In another of the short lyrics from his second book he moves from pain to wonder. This is the entirety of "Lyric 12":

I believe in myself slowly.
It takes all of the doubts I've got.
It takes my wonder.

This is marvelous economy. I love the way doubt and wonder are put together here. It is so easy to forget that they are really rooted in the same not-knowingness. It reminds us too that all of the actions in this small poem—believing, doubting and wondering—are actions, of course, whose end-goals are their root nouns, and which take work to accomplish. The present tense of this poem suggests that it, like the awareness I alluded to earlier, is daily work. We must work at wonder, and work out our doubting, and work at believing. It is when we forget to do those things that we get stuck in the other kind of not-knowing: ignorance. So it is with race, I think. The more we presume to ignore (there's that word again, the action this time) of race in the communities around us, the less of ourselves we see. Who, when you walk down the street, do you look in the eye? Who do you smile at? What will our children see? Can they see me? I wonder.

Anger is maybe most useful when it is turned inwards. There really can be no righteous anger unless the self is implicated. Otherwise, it is merely self-righteous, and the difference between righteousness and self-righteousness is perhaps the difference between a telescope and a mirror, one a way of seeing, the other a reflection of what you already knew. So, as St. John suggests in the poems above, if we are going to help our children think usefully about race, they must understand that they also are implicated. Too often, I think, we act as if children were perfect vessels of innocence who can somehow "choose" to see color or not, or distrust other people, have faith, etc. But they begin the process of becoming themselves as soon as they are born. Like all of us, our children, even as young as Lois, our five-year-old, have preconceptions, underlying biases and preferences. What makes them different from us is that they tend to be more willing to acknowledge those things. So the more we can be angry with ourselves, angry at our failure to be better people, the more our kids too will understand that that sort of thing is a process. Kids are not born "good"—they are born people, who are paradoxes, imperfect and always in need of work, just like the families and communities they are born into.

Here's Primus St. John one more time, from his unfinished long poem, "If There Were No Days, Where Would We Live," on the dangers of not recognizing our preconceptions:

I am near that elaborate house
where all the people killed themselves.
They said they were angels
on their way back home.
I can understand how it feels
to want the hand of God to hold onto
when it's excruciatingly painful,
but it is also true
that all the angels are gone
and we are the women and the men

that they've left
with only each other's hands
to hold onto.

In a marvelous reconceptualization of faith, St. John at once denies these true believers their present angels, while still admitting the angels' past existence. He does not decry the faith itself, but just where it is placed. In the image of a cultish suicide, we see a metaphor for any understanding that leaves out the self's true complicity—be it facile thinking on race, on rights, on poverty, etc.—when we ignore the self, its true power can be erased. And while it is true that theologians and mystics of various stripes have argued for the negation of the self, it is almost always in the context of understanding the self as part of a larger community, so the self is not erased but subsumed, or sublimated. We are not meant to leave the world, but to join it. And that is exactly what St. John wants for us here as well—that we can't put trust in ideas only, but the ways those ideas are rooted in the physical bodies of the people around us. No prayer, no poem, is as strong as a held hand, he seems to say. And is there any better place to practice this challenge than in a family? We must model the erasure not of the self, but of the *us* and *them* St. John wrote about in "Dreamer." Though, of course, it will be an imperfect erasure. We will not reach the understanding we seek; we will not fully impart to our kids why our communities are fractured and how to fix them, but we can keep the nouns in our sights, can reach out for whatever hands might be there to hold and just try to hold them.

What Do We Ask of Ourselves?
(2017)

In space it is cold. Just a little warmer than what is known as absolute zero—a phrase that has always sounded to me like it comes from a David Bowie or Marvin Gaye song, not science, and is really as much a concept as anything else: the infinite of cold, the full-on hard-to-conceive-of absence of warmth. And yet, we stare out at that void each night—if you are lucky enough to live somewhere where you can see past the lights—transfixed by the possibility of absence, of that that is most surely not us.

My son Rache has recently come out of a black hole phase (and has regrettably entered a seemingly horizonless Pokémon phase . . .). But for a while there he was interested in almost nothing else—we had the library's entire collection of black hole related books, he was on internet astronomy sites trying to see if there were any pictures of black holes (I pointed out that that seemed somewhat impossible—though I have since been proven otherwise). In their absence he drew his own pictures, made little mini science fair presentation posters, asked me over and over again whether a person could go into a black hole. His idea was that if you were to make an armored suit out of dark matter, you'd be safe in there. I told him I hoped that would be the case should he find himself in one.

But I don't want him, or anyone, in the universe's black holes. We've got enough of them here on earth, I'd say. As Frost so rightly foresees in his terrifying poem "Desert Places"—the unearthly is an apt metaphor for the earthly. Even when we send actual people into actual space, we read the journey as a kind of metaphor for our own searching. Isn't that why the space tragedies—Challenger, Columbia—of my life have been such major tragedies? A part of our own dreaming, of our own sense of being, went with them. In those instances, the cold void won out (as deep down we always suspect it will).

The essential American poet Robert Hayden thinks about the metaphorical (and metaphysical) conundrum of space in his late poem "Astronauts." I read this poem to Rache during the black hole phase—when I was telling him about the moon landing. Here's the whole thing:

ASTRONAUTS

Armored in oxygen,
       faceless in visors—
mirrormasks reflecting
         the mineral glare and
shadow of moonscape—
        they walk slowmotion
floatingly the lifeless
        dust of Taurus
Littrow. And Wow, they
       exclaim; oh boy, this is it.

       They sing, exulting
(though trained to be wary
       of "emotion and
philosophy"), breaking
       the calcined stillness
of once Absolute Otherwhere.

Risking edges, earthlings
       to whom only
their machines are friendly
       (and God's radar—
watching eye?), they
       labor at gathering
proof of hypothesis;
       in snowshine of sunlight
dangerous as radium
       probe detritus for clues.

>   *What is it we wish them*
> *to find for us, as*
>   *we watch them on our*
> *screens? They loom there*
>   *heroic antiheroes,*
> *smaller than myth and*
>   *poignantly human.*
> *Why are we troubled?*
>   *What do we ask of these men?*
> *What do we ask of ourselves?*

There's so much to consider here, so many things happening at once. Hayden was a poet who masterfully oscillated between form and free-verse, often blurring the lines between the two, and in this poem we see all sorts of lines being blurred—between forms, between earth and space, between the human and the non-human, between god and no god. The titular astronauts themselves, I think, we must see as liminal figures, potential guides, meant to show us a way across strange and frightening lines.

And to serve that function Hayden has to prepare them. As with my son's dark matter suit—Hayden's voyagers are armored in the first line of the poem, not in plastic and rubber, but with the oxygen they need to breathe. Their very earthliness is what will not only sustain but protect, their human faces obscured by the beautiful and terrifying "mirrormasks" they must wear. We, the earthbound observers, look at their faces and only see our own. They are protected, in a way, by us and our desires and hopes for them. And, as they shuffle through the dust, the weight of our world (or worldlessness) is on their shoulders, as it were, and they look up and language fails them. This is my favorite moment of the poem, where Hayden abandons the lyric impulse, because no lyric will do. The plain dumfounded nothingness of the linguistic response shows our inability to express real wonder. And Wow. Or maybe that is the only way to wonder.

• • •

As I was beginning this essay, in mid-2017, a racist rally took place in Charlottesville, VA, just up the road from where I live. There were white supremacists in battle gear, not mirrormasks, some fully armed; there was violence and confrontation, many were injured, one young woman was killed. Robert Hayden spent his career writing and thinking about the way race dominates our culture and the ways we allow it to dominate our culture. Hayden taught for many years at Fisk University in Nashville—a historically black college. His long poem, "Middle Passage," is one of the defining artistic inquiries on American slavery. The book that "Astronauts" comes from, American Journal, is an extended attempt to document Americanness through poems—and it opens and closes with poems specifically addressing race and humanity. One doesn't need to wonder what Hayden would have thought of the rally in Charlottesville. Oh Wow, he might have said.

We see in this event, and others like it, the thing we always knew was there. Just as the astronauts in the poem knew the earth was there, knew more or less what it looked like, to actually see it reorders their (and our) sense of what we know and knew. Except, of course, in their case the awe was rooted in beauty, some terror surely, but mostly beauty. In the case of the display of hatred and purposeful violence I saw in Charlottesville, the awe is a similar emotion, but rooted fully in fear and horror. And later, when the astronauts, though cautioned against "emotion and philosophy," start singing, we can't help but hear their awestruck and terrorstruck voices mingle weirdly with our own.

Which, of course, is exactly what we need now. More singing, but in this instance an angry kind. More loud declarations of awe. Hayden knows in this poem that what we see in these astronauts are travelers who know how to handle an alien landscape. They are doing it for us. They are enacting human endeavor in our stead. Like Christ, in the Christian tradition, dying so the world does not have to, these astronauts—now made fully symbol—are showing us how to move in uncertainty and fear by doing it for us. We are to sing; loudly with purpose.

For many Americans, I think, talking about race feels like an Absolute Otherwhere. Two days after the rally, I was at a community band rehearsal (I play the tuba) and happened that evening to be wearing a Black Lives Matter t-shirt. I like wearing the shirt in my small rural town; it gives me a sense of what it might feel like to have everyone notice your outward appearance at every stage of the day (something that white Americans don't often feel). I am under no illusion that it is any kind of a divestiture of or atonement for my white privilege—that is still forever and lamentably intact—but the shirt does become a kind of small empathic tool for me, and it is interesting to notice people's reactions to it. I live in a divided southern town, and there are certainly some glares when I wear the shirt, but there are an equal number of those inclined to smile or make a positive comment. But at the community band rehearsal—probably one of the most quintessentially Rockwellian and democratic sorts of weekly gatherings one could find in America—as I was putting away my music stand, I was approached by a new member, accosted really, about the shirt.

It was a predictable encounter in many ways. You probably see it coming. He wanted to know if I didn't think that all lives matter. I pointed out the obvious, that, in fact, that is exactly what the shirt suggests—that certain lives, black lives in this case, have *not* heretofore been shown by our society to matter as much as others. But he was insistent, all the while declaring his lack of racism, that to say that black lives matter is to say that other lives don't matter as much. In fact, he said, strangely, that that is what the shirt said. I literally looked down at the three words on my shirt and asked him where it said that, and he looked back at me bewildered, still insisting that that's what it meant.[1]

Our conversation then spiraled into my fellow bandmember's nearly shouting his fear-filled beliefs about Black Americans during the Obama years and what they did and didn't deserve. All the while I tried hard to stay calm and refute his obvious falsehoods. But there was another part of my mind which was detached from the conversation, which floated like a moonman above it in a way, watching and noting how unprepared I was. I could have used a dark matter suit or some special oxygen to keep me focused and to keep my footsteps safe. I was in awe. Awe that we're still having this sort of conversation, awe that I was having to have it (released from my comfortable bubble, my spaceship of Whiteness and routine and familiar people), awe that this man was literally unable to conceive of the simple meaning of the three words on my shirt. His interaction

---

1. I'd like to add here, that I hope no reader takes this essay to be my own proclamation of having somehow transcended racism. As do most of us, I have persistent work to do to look past my privileges and internalized biases.

with race was so otherworldly, that he couldn't see it. It would be like Hayden's astronauts standing on the moon, looking out at earth and saying, "Well, that must not be it."

And, ironically, of course, many conspiracy theories have existed to explain away the fact of the moon landing, just as we concoct theories to explain away the facts of systemic racism in our American society. However, the simple fact remains: men walked on the moon, there are flags and footprints there to prove it. Also: the descendants of an enslaved people (freed only 2–3 generations before I was born) have far fewer advantages than the descendants of those who enslaved them. This is not an opinion, but an economic, historical, and sociological fact. My band colleague argued that we need to forget history and move on. My private moonman, hovering above me, was too dispassionate to make me say that it is history that won't let us go, not the other way around. If we were to "move on" from history, we would be willing to abolish all legacies of slavery, like underfunded schools, the electoral college, unmet promises of land and capital, and many more. But that's not what he meant. And even that wouldn't be moving on, just finally recognizing something, that each of those things are both present day facts affecting us, and a part of our history. History and the present will always have an uncomfortable resemblance, and narrative ties. We get all the way to the moon, and it is round and rocky and connected inextricably to earth.

As Hayden points out in the latter part of the poem, the men on the moon, in turn, were inextricably connected to us. There's a passage in *Moby Dick* where Melville, in the voice of his narrator Ishmael, observes that always our "own individuality [is] merged in a joint stock company," that like it or not, "every mortal that breathes" is connected to "a plurality of other mortals." He concludes the observation—after noting how the slightest slip from a banker or a pharmacist could send you to ruin—by reminding himself that no matter what, in regards to the rope that binds us all we always only have "the management of one end of it." It is an important passage—not only because it reminds us of how much we rely on one another, but also, how much responsibility that connection brings with it. It is both a fact of existence and one of its privileges to need so many others and for them to need us. To be an individual is a paradox, because an individual human only makes sense in the context of a community. Monks live both alone and together. We are isolated in our skin, but connected through and through by the bonds of society and love.

What my band colleague couldn't understand is that it is in *our own* self-interest to be sure that other human lives matter. And if a certain type of life has been devalued, unmattered, for the past two-hundred years and more, then we have a responsibility to redress that sin. It is only to our benefit that we properly manage our end of the rope. It is no accident that in that passage in *Moby Dick*, Ishmael, a white sailor, is connected by the rope to Queequeg, a Pacific Islander.[2] Here, in the starkest terms, Melville shows us the same racial or, writ larger, human, situation we are in today. Ishmael has a responsibility to get Queequeg safely back on board the ship, standing next to him. As do we.

• • •

In the third and quietest stanza of "Astronauts," Hayden has us just watch the moonwalkers moonwalk around doing experiments, ducking the eye of God and trying hard to learn something. But the diction of the poem suggests futility—they are "laboring" to prove what they think they know, they can trust only their machines, sun looks like snow, and by the end the astronauts are almost resignedly poking in the dust like kids who have run out of ideas. All the while we are watching them. And if we follow Melville, they are connected directly to us—maybe, in a weird way, watching us too, watching us watch them search for us, do the heavy lifting of awe.

Let's go back to the parenthetical in that stanza for a minute. Hayden is also one of the more interesting American poets when it comes to faith. He has something in common with John Donne—furious at times with God, but always finding a place to let him into the work. Here we're not sure what to make of "God's radar—/watching eye." It is such a fascinating line break—at first God is just one of the machines, a radar we can trust in, but then after the enjambment we are lost in a bit of a syntactical mystery: is God watching the radar (so merely keeping track of the astronauts)? Or is his eye itself a radar, probing the human world, seeing our messy movements? Either way, it is Hayden's reminder to himself that

2. All of this is from Ch. 72 ("The Monkey-Rope") of Melville's novel.

even despite this incredible human moment—man's first step on a celestial body, there is always something bigger than us to consider.

And maybe that detached observer—the sense of a God's eye hovering over us—is a better way to describe that feeling I had talking to my bandmate, the feeling maybe we have when talking to anyone about these Otherwheres that dog us. To that observer I felt a responsibility to get the interaction right, as if I might only have that chance, which to some extent is true. In each interaction with another human, we have responsibilities: responsibilities to represent ourselves truthfully, to represent those of whom we speak truthfully, and to show love. Now we are going to fail at these things, but the ideal seems unquestionable to me. So Hayden, to me, in that moment—reminding us of God's radar—is reminding us too of the ways responsibility never leaves us behind. Many writers have described freedom as more of a responsibility than a liberty, and I think that is true. There is greater ease in having your decisions made for you. But here, where we feel free, we must constantly work towards, are bound by, our ideals.

It is towards that kind of thinking that Hayden takes us in the end of his beautiful poem. I could have picked a much more likely poem for thinking about race—much of Hayden's work explicitly explores the topic—but in this poem, I am just so moved by the way he gets at the real questions that difficult things ask us: "Why are we troubled?," "What do we ask of ourselves?" As the astronauts explore the moon, on *our* screens the poet points out, we know that they are also exploring the farther reaches of human responsibility. They are treading not, it turns out, where we merely cannot go ourselves, but where we are afraid to go. In 1969, when these men first stepped onto the lunar surface, the country was also in uncharted social territory. A post-Civil Rights world might as well have been the moon. So what in God's name were we to do? We see this so clearly in his description of the astronauts as mere men: "smaller than myth and / poignantly human," so enough like us for us to understand the responsibility. There is no moral here, no resolved quest. This is a first foot out.

And here we are now in the ageing early twenty-first century, not gone back to the actual moon but still adrift on that other moon of our own making. We've had a president who seemed unaware of, or hostile to, the advances of the 1960s and 70s, much less those of the Obama years.

We have a divided media which literally has to wrestle itself to convince viewers of what is simple fact and what is utterly made-up. Now I am not so naïve as to think that fabrication has not always played a role in media, but without some kind of centralized trust—so basic trust in basic institutions: news organizations, core government functions, universities, each other—it feels difficult, as a community, to hold onto any shared values.

When I came to the next band rehearsal, the wife of the man who had accosted me kindly handed me an envelope bearing what she said was an apology letter from her husband. She told me he had been remorseful of his anger ever since our encounter at the last rehearsal—I joked that it was easy to get mad at a tuba player and took the package. When I got home later that evening and read the letter, I found a neat hand-written note indeed apologizing, but mostly also just further explaining why I was, still, wrong to have been wearing the Black Lives Matter shirt. The letter angrily and familiarly accused Black Lives Matter of organizing riots and promoting violence against police officers, of which, of course there is absolutely no evidence. White nationalist groups, like the ones in Charlottesville, march with weapons and combat gear and in their promotional materials support violent uprising. Black Lives Matter and affiliated groups have never done anything of the sort. Protest, yes; violence, no.

But it was more the tone of the letter that I found so dispiriting. Is an apology still an apology if it's mostly an explanation of why someone shouldn't have to apologize? "What do we ask of ourselves?" Hayden wants to know, and I fear the answer is often very little. How many of us even remember to listen to that detached voice, the one hovering above us, tentatively poking along our own private screens? I hope to God, and his radar-watching eye, that I can learn to listen better and to convince my kids to do the same. "What do we ask of ourselves?" The question really asks us to admit to our own unknowingness. And when we don't know things, trust in love and positive forces is our best path forward. Saying that lives matter is a positive thing. Being offended that someone might think that is, simply and clearly, negative. If we push ourselves towards community, instead of pulling further back into ourselves, we will see the responsibility of freedom for what it is: a beautiful, deep-set, footstep into an Otherwhere we've only, before now, imagined.

And, to be honest, I can see how someone might give into the pull of being a believer in race divisions or being pro-life, or against gender equality, etc. These things make the surface look simple—panaceas or magic fixes, simple organizing criteria for an otherwise complex world. If only that one thing could change, things would "return" to normal, as nostalgists often have it. And doesn't Hayden address this very idea in his poem? At the top of the last stanza he asks "What is it we wish them / to find for us"—as if maybe in this brave exploration they will find the thing we have lost, the key to America that we surely once had. Somehow it got lost on the moon! we'd say. How funny, I'm sure glad those guys went up to get it for us. But no, of course, the key is here in us all along, which Hayden also knows. "Why are we troubled?" he wants to know. Because we know where the key is. We have so much trouble admitting when things are more complicated than we can grasp. Notice that Hayden has no answers to his questions, just more questions.

So I watch Robert Hayden move through this poem the way he watches his titular explorers tread across the moon, his alternately indented lines like awkward footsteps moving down the page. It is easy, as I have done through this essay and others, to turn to poets for answers, to ask them what it is we are supposed to think about things, how to understand the world. It is maybe too easy for me, a white reader, to turn to this Black poet and churlishly ask for answers about race. I mean no harm, of course, but the harm might be even just in the assumptions behind my asking. But here in this late poem, Hayden is a step ahead of me, turning the poem kindly back on me, pointing out that I have really come here to ask questions not of the poem, or of him, but of myself. What I love about this poem, in the end, is the way it turns all of its readers into explorers, venturing into our own inner strangenesses. I stare up at the moon. I stare into the faces of my neighbors. I stare into my fellow band-member's angry argument. I stare into mirrors. I am lost in all of those places. But I can still try to explore them despite my fear. I can take my oxygen and look squarely at the beauty that is everywhere to be found, in everyone, and say, to whomever might be watching—the radar eye, my kids, my moonman, you—this is it.

The Wondering Child

Elizabeth Coatsworth and the Unexpected
(2018)

In this life we wait and want for things. We hope for things. In short, we expect. We expect children. We expect certain things to happen. We tell people what to expect. We expect the Food Lion to have mediocre tomatoes. We expect Mrs. Tilson will get better soon, or that she might not. We expect the sun to rise a little later. We expect our daughter home at any minute. We expect the news to come any day now. You probably have expectations for this essay, even, that it will do something on the order of what other essays do. And maybe it will. But how could I know what you are expecting?

There are ways in which managing expectations is one of the key parts of living. We try to figure out what the day will bring, we try to make sure our kids aren't disappointed. Kids, in fact, and famously, have some of our more outrageous sets of expectations. Toddlers do not like it when things turn out a way they didn't expect: if a sandwich arrives for lunch cut in triangles instead of rectangles, or if the toothpaste is suddenly a new flavor. And maybe the shock of surprise is built into us from that early age, but we also learn to enjoy things we don't expect—a full moon we didn't know about, a beer in the back of the fridge, a huge Japanese squash hiding in the vines. Our expectations define our days to some extent—and the way we form them perhaps plays an important role in how we inhabit space in the world. I'd like to teach my children to cherish both the expected and the unexpected, though the latter makes for a harder task.

One way I like to challenge my own expectations is to read a new old writer. It is fun to read the newest, youngest, upandcomingest writers, of course, but I find I come to them perhaps most full of expectation and not all of them always good.[1] To seek a true surprise, I like to dig up writers that are, in ways, forgotten—writers from the 19th or early 20th century (or earlier) who had notable careers, but whom no one seems to think about much anymore. Longfellow is in this camp to some extent (who we've already discussed) and George Scarbrough. But I want to turn for this piece to an even less-acknowledged writer than that—Elizabeth Coatsworth. Coatsworth was well-known as a children's writer, publishing dozens of books over a long life of writing (she died in 1986 at the age of 93). She was married to the nature writer Henry Beston, and both of them were known for their literary devotion to coastal New England.

But Coatsworth began her writing career with poems. Her first book, *Fox Footprints*, was published by Knopf in 1923. It is, as is her second book, a book of travel poems—in this case mostly to Japan and China. Here's a poem from the Japan section of the book:

REMINISCENCE

It is a holiday, and shall be casually used
As fits its dignity.
I will wander among Japanese silks
Piled here beside me on the window-seat,
Stray squares of fancy
Sold in the low close-packed Kyoto streets.
Here are ultramarine rivers
With long skeins of foam
On which float boats laden with flowers;
Here are symbols
On gamboge—pine, bamboo, heron and tortoise
Auguring an old age or a happy married life;
And there a flock of fat-cheeked flying sparrows
In browns and grays and dullest granite-blues
Flood a whole square of mauve and violet—
The soft silk almost flutters with their wings;
And next come fancies to entice a child:

---

1. This is, to be clear, my problem and not theirs.

The black hare of the moon, pounding elixir,
The jeweled orange crow that nests in the sun,
And then my favorite, three round parasol-tops
Jostling together while brocaded leaves
Float down upon them—there is the whole scene—
The pith of autumn! scarlet wizardry
Soft-tapping on the dull brown parasols
Which hide invisible bright faces. . . .
Idly I turn the squares
Each one the marrow of some delicate mood.

This is a marvelous poem, presaging in its wry demeanor Elizabeth Bishop's first book (or maybe, more accurately, her second book), which wouldn't be published for decades. Coatsworth splits her time pretty evenly in this volume between formal poems and free verse, which we see on display here. However, this poem, like in much free verse of the time, rises often to iambic pentameter (see the powerful effect in the fourth, sixteenth and final line, as examples). The formal backdrop gives the voice a kind of off-handed authority, which fits, as well, the "casual" (to borrow her word) tone of the poem. And this is a poem that is about both the expected and the unexpected. The first two lines set a mood that is hard to pin down. Is the speaker being sarcastic about the "dignity" of the holiday? Or is she dignifying casualness? It's not entirely clear, and she wants us not to know exactly what to expect as we go forward in the poem.

The speaker herself (and I am presuming a female speaker here) is searching her own expectations. As she looks out the window, her attention turns to the fabric samples stacked next to her. She feels her way through them (the tactile imagery of Bishop's later "yard-goods" comes to mind) and allows herself to be surprised. She seems bored by the world both inside and outside the window but enthralled by the fictional worlds of the fabric designs—their cogency and seeming simplicity perhaps. The gamboge, saffron-yellow of the Buddhist monk, is filled with animals, the moon is a rabbit or a rabbit is the moon, sparrows become the silk itself. I love her description of the final fabric: "there is the whole scene" she says with surprise almost (and is that exclamation mark in the next line ironic or not?). Red leaves fall on parasols—with people, who we presume to be happy, hidden beneath them, unexpected in their sequestered brightness. Even the poet can't quite describe the emotion of the scene, and so backs out of the poem with that marvelous last line—asking us to focus on those surprising words, "marrow" and "delicate," which the meter highlights and, for me, pull us back to the image of the speaker gazing languidly out of her holiday window, with nothing else to do, nothing much else to expect.

How many days do we start idly like this? Putting on our running shoes, turning on the shower. We think ahead to what the day requires of us, but we don't always think about what exactly the day will bring. Such an approach would require, really, a rewiring of our busy western ways of being. Coatsworth seems to intuit this in the poem—the Japanese fabric, in ways, stands in for another way of seeing. But I love how in this carefully honest poem, the speaker is not fundamentally changed. This is not a sappy poem (as others in the collection are) about the transports of travelling in the East. This is a poem that notes how our expectations can be quietly shattered, but we *still* go back to our set ways, our starting approaches.

Yesterday I took the dogs for a walk with Lois. She loves to come on the morning walk with me, though she never remembers how much she loves it until I'm just about to leave—often setting off a furious search for pants, shoes, etc. while the dogs stand around expectant and impatient with their leashes already on. When we finally got out the door, I was already thinking of the day ahead. I think of walking the dogs as one of my "tasks" in the morning—I have to go for a run, open the chicken coop, water plants in the little greenhouse, feed the dogs and take them for a walk. I can't sit down and relax until all of that is done, and so I often forward-think my way through it. The dogs are both thirteen, so even getting them down the house stairs to eat and down the porch stairs for the walk is becoming a bigger challenge. So all of this was on my mind, and I droned though the task. We made it about ten steps before the frailer dog, Sutton, decided he didn't want to walk down the driveway, and tugged Lois to go toward our neighbor's field instead. I decided to let him have his way, and we walked the field-road that winds between rain-high corn and a hilly cow pasture. As we moved along in the shadowless heat (one reason I didn't want to go this way), Lois and I together and at once heard an unusual chirping above us and saw what I realized was a small group of swallows feeding above the corn. I love swallows. And not having any real outbuildings nearby, I rarely see them here. I was elated to watch them swerve and dive and to point out their famous tails to Lois. They allowed us to stand there for maybe a minute before they moved further out into the field.

We turned around and headed back home (the dogs can't go too far in the heat) soon after, and in making sure the dogs did what they were supposed to out there, keeping Lois far enough away from the electric fence, and thinking about what else needed to happen that day, I forgot about the swallows by the time we got back home. Lois, however, burst through the door and ran into the sewing room to tell my wife Kate all about them. She had allowed the unexpected to make a good-sized indentation in her morning, whereas I had allowed it to bounce off almost undetected. I'm not saying we shouldn't plan our days, and get needed things done—but there was something in Lois' use of that moment that seems better than mine. This morning, when we took the dogs again, she asked, unprompted, if we could go see the neat birds again. I wasn't expecting her to ask that, either.

. . .

One definition of travel , one could argue, would be to *seek out* the unexpected. As Emerson notes in "Self-Reliance," of course, that doesn't always work out so well, but Coatsworth made a good go at it. And while in Japan sitting in that window she may not have learned what to do with the unexpected, she keeps seeking it out in her second book, *Atlas and Beyond*, from 1924. Here's a short poem from a section on Italy:

ALL GOATS

All goats have a wild-brier grace
They are as elegant as thorns
With little bells beneath their chins
And pointed horns.

So quick are they upon their feet,
So light and gaily do they prance

Their hoofs seem sportive castanets
To which they dance.

And as they raise sagacious heads
Disturbed by some crude passer-by
They gaze upon him with a most
Satiric eye.

So much to like about this little poem—it is light, yes, but hides a kind of seriousness as well. It is serious, most notably, in the music of the first stanza. This poem is in an iambic 4442 metrical pattern within its quatrains—but there would be no way of knowing what kind of meter you are in for by just reading the first line, it could scan as having three or four stresses. The double stress sound on "wild-brier" upends any kind of normative iambic reading of the line (without, at least, a regular line to serve as a barometer). So in this moment where the goats are introduced, the music of the poem is similarly wild. Things even out after that metrically, but Coatsworth has succeeded in stripping the reader of any normal set of expectations in that first line. And then there is the semantic dissonance in the second line's simile—the surprisingly beautiful notion of the thorn as something elegant is so out of keeping with what we expect in a "charming" little light poem like this, that one almost has to reread the line. The writing is maybe not quite as fabulous in the other two stanzas—but I enjoy the way the humans in the poem are "crude" and the nearly fully anthropomorphized goat has the upper hand of wisdom. The goats, in Coatsworth's hands, are so unexpected that the passers-by don't even know what to make of them. Maybe we readers don't know quite what to make of this poet either.

The watching and understanding we see in "All Goats" sets the tone for a lot of this book. Coatsworth the traveler is determined to find the unexpected in her subjects and images. Here's what might be the best poem in the volume, also set in Italy:

THE GLASS TOPPED COACH

(18TH CENTURY)

The yellow leaves drift from the sycamores
As though the fresco of Autumn were peeling
In wide flakes of gold from a painted ceiling,
And the smoke of fires sifts thin and bland
Among the poplars, while haze and dreams
Come sumptuously over the sapless land.
A great coach lurches along the road
With round-necked horses and straight-backed grooms
And between gilt cupids and curling swans
The coats-of-arms as grand as on tombs.
Ah happy coach like an autumn rose
And safely curled in your crested heart
Art that is Man, Man that is Art!

The horses' hoofs drum along the ground
And the gold coach sways in a world of gold
And from the city before them sound
The welcoming four-o'clock bells . . . . roll on
Garlanded coach with your top of glass!
The Autumn day is nearing its crown
When easy and gracious, with silk knees crossed
Your master shall take his snuff and stare
At the girls who sit in the windows there
Smiling above him and looking down.
A flower may drop on your roof of glass
And the streets will sound to the roll of your wheels
As in a triumph of love you pass.

The great coach vanishes, gold amid gold,
Gorgeous and brittle along the road.

This poem really surprised me when I found it (if it were a little weirder and had some rum-timma-tums in it, it could be a deep cut from

Wallace Stevens): the title itself is more whimsical than most, the historical setting equally unexpected. Formally, this poem is rhymed, but without a set pattern, in strange stanzas of thirteen lines with a concluding couplet. Metrically it is in iambic tetrameter, but with so many anapests (at least one per line), that they tint the sonic character of the poem entirely. The meter itself seems to be like the weirdly ostentatious and out-of-place carriage jostling its way down the road. The poem in ways feels like a sibling to "Reminiscence," with its ekphrastic look at fabric patterns. This one might be an ekphrastic poem masquerading as a historical one—the image it conveys becomes the entirety of the poem, until late in the second stanza. She drops clues to this idea with the early simile of autumn itself as a fresco, but it is more the way the image commands the page. I love where "the smoke of fires sifts thin and bland," the weird word "sifts," high and weak in the mouth, not only allows for a strange-feeling iamb there in the line but sets up the stretched feel of the subsequent adverbs. Similarly, in the second stanza, the line "And the gold coach sways in a world of gold" is just marvelous—the unabashed repetition of the adjective drives home the real haughtiness mixed with real beauty that the poem embodies.

And then, of course, we get to the odd centerpiece of the poem—the impotent silk-bedecked owner of this fantastic coach. He feels slightly creepy as he peers from his weird assemblage "At the girls who sit in the windows there," or that at least is how we read it at first. But something about the way they look at him and let him pass also suggests that it is he who we end up pitying here. That "triumph of love" feels like it could be self-love or, at best, simply a nostalgic love for things passing and past, but, either way, the coach rolls through town, "brittle," inconsequential, beautiful and gone. And, finally, note that, as in "Reminiscence," it is the inanimate object that gets the real attention in the poem. The poem is an apostrophe to the coach itself, an elegy, a praising of its existence perhaps, but, either way, a preference on the part of the poet for the ideal—the figured thing, not the people who surround it. The women in the windows of this poem (we think, of course, of the speaker of "Reminiscence" here), stare down, but assuming a glare, probably only see the jewel-shine of the glass. The man behind it is hidden in its brightness, which, like all lovely things, is inaccessible and ephemeral. In the end, this is a dark and impressive Modern poem.

Elizabeth Coatsworth spent most of the latter part of her life on a coastal farm in Maine, known as Chimney Farm. She and her husband, Henry Beston, bought the property without seeing it, somehow knowing it would be the place they would root themselves for good. It is interesting to see a poet who so defined herself by travelling in her first two books of poems turn to anchoring herself to a specific place. Coatsworth's fourth book of poems, *Country Poems*, reflects that transition by containing almost no travelling poems—it is instead a Frost-inspired meditation on the rural life. We'll get to that book by the end here, so hang on. But investigating Coatsworth's life for this piece made me think about my own situation—and with that word I mean the literal place I am situated in. I bought my nine acres here in southcentral Virginia having only seen it once. And when I saw it, it had a beautiful green lawn, a nice smallish house, and a long half-mile driveway that snakes by a meadow down to the road. Good enough.

When we drove up that driveway a few weeks later to meet the moving truck, our three-month old first baby and two young dogs in tow, we found nine acres that hadn't seen rain in a while. All that green grass was completely brown (it had been, obviously, a quick-growing rye that had run its course), the meadow was crispy and low, the house stood in the blazing sun with only a few young trees nearby; there were no outbuildings, no shade, no flowers, no gardens. It was as alien as a new homeplace could possibly be upon arrival. Not, needless to say, what we remembered or expected. The first thing I bought here was a tiller, and we got to work. I remember planting my first perennials in the clay, with a posthole digger

Ten years later I look out my window at that same stretch of land, and it is all changed. The rye grass is gone, replaced by a mostly-reliably green carpet of native weeds. There are large vegetable gardens filled too with flowers—Mexican sunflowers and zinnias mostly. There is a stand of blueberries, an arbor of muscadines, an unstoppable municipality of thornless blackberries, a chicken yard, much larger trees, and flower beds haphazarded around the yard like volcanic islands. Everything here now marks and records our presence, along with, of course, the constant presence of our neighbors—voles, foxes, woodpeckers, deer, skunks, goldeneye ducks, bears, raccoons, herons, etc. So sometimes the unexpected comes at a slow burn. The difference between our place now and our place then is startling—but it has come just from living. The small decisions you make—let's put a butterfly bush here, let's move the crepe myrtles there, let's do some roses—impact your surroundings for years. Is this kind of thing planning or, like travel, courting the unexpected? I like to think of it as the latter; it's more fun.

And all of this is to point out that one doesn't have to travel or actively seek out the unexpected. It is everywhere around us. We could call it the push of time, or God, or the force of change, or any number of things—but, in the end, the unexpected reminds us that our efforts only play into the larger vectors that push the world along. And perhaps this is most noticeable when we stay in one place for a while. In her strange third book of poems, *Compass Rose*, which is hard to find, Coatsworth is transitioning from being a traveler to a stayer.[2] There are poems about far-flung places (notably New Mexico in this book), and her first poems about country life (there is a poem about the new Maine farm at the end). There are also poems that fit into neither category. Take "Portrait," for example:

Distinguished as fretted iron,
Immovable, subtle, relentless,
He upholds the cult of moulds,—
Everything which has hardened into forms,
All that has crystallized into sharp outline:
He is fanatic in defence of the ponderable past.
Calm, smiling, and icily in earnest
He matches his strength against the full oncoming force of change.

Maybe Coatsworth was already forseeing the change in her own writing that was coming, her transition to a different kind of poetry—she would publish only one more volume of poems for adults after this book—or indeed the transition from poetry to children's writing. But in this poem we might see what happens when we refuse to acknowledge the unexpected things time will bring. The subject of this poem is a prow pointed backwards, but still moving forwards despite its intentions. And look how wonderfully Coatsworth mimics (mocks?) this in the form of the

---

2. The book was published in 1929, a year when many good books were buried by circumstance (perhaps like 2020).

poem. This unrhymed poem begins in iambic trimeter, but after the third line shifts to a very loose pentameter, with the final line bursting out to seven feet (reminiscent perhaps of hymn meter or the old fourteener). In short, the poem presents itself as metrical, but exploding out towards a freer kind of verse—the "oncoming force of change," perhaps. Coatsworth herself seems indifferent to the winds of poetic change, writing as she does in both form and free verse, but she is merciless in mocking the man at the center of this poem. And, moving beyond the meter here, we see a portrait of a person we do not want to become. "The cult of moulds" should be our new euphemism for social media, and we should always beware of "hardening into forms." Coatsworth, in this wonderful and tough little poem, is asking us always to be alive to what is alive around us—the expected and the unexpected, the things time has brought us, and the things it has yet to bring.

• • •

I bought *Country Poems*, Elizabeth Coatsworth's fourth and, in ways, final book of poems strictly for adult readers, long before I had the others. I bought it when I was working on my own book of country poems. I too had recently moved to a remote place. I too was writing rhymes about growing things, keeping animals, family, neighbors, etc. I found the poems, when they weren't sometimes surprisingly excellent, always charming. There is a comfortable settled sort of air about them. I found my copy at a used bookstore on Cary St. in Richmond, VA and bought it based on the title alone, so I had no idea what to expect. But what I found was a sympathetic voice, someone who trusted that poems were sturdy and useful and who trusted that they might teach her something about a place. Here is one small example to wrap things up with:

PASTORAL

Before the lamps are lighted,
Before the west is dark,
When song awakes the wood-thrush
And silences the lark,

When even meadow daisies
Grow dim beside the lane
And the small wind of evening
Moves with a sound like rain,

The horses in the pasture
Drift slowly to the bars
Advancing on the wondering child
Their foreheads, blazed with stars.

The poem, in ways, sums up a lot of what I've been trying to say about the unexpected and this unexpectedly excellent writer. And how ironic that this questing and travelling poet had to settle down somewhere to say it. The entire poem has the feel of noticing to it. It is, again, about a liminal time—the time between day and night, the brief space when it is dark but not yet dark enough for added light. We hear that in the first stanza, and then the wondering begins. The poet marvels, with that word "even" in the fifth line, that the bright snow-white daisies have begun to lower their wattage in the dusk. The wind is surprising and unfamiliar enough to warrant the poem's only simile. Then, finally, we have the central image of the poem—the children "wondering" at the celestial horses. Coatsworth marks the centrality of this line by adding a fourth foot in a poem of otherwise perfectly regular trimeter. Our metrical expectation is firmly established in the ear by this point in the poem, so the extra foot surprises us as much as the horses surprise the child. And in line with the metrical gesture, the image is weirder than it might at first seem. One reading has the child beckoning actual horses in the pasture, but another might have the sky itself, the oncoming darkness, *as* a kind of horse. So the horses become the metaphor and the stars their true selves. In either reading, the child is seeing something extraordinary, that he or she didn't expect. Something natural is paired with something almost supernatural: horses with their heads aflame, a night sky charging down.

The world, in this supposedly quiet pastoral, is suffused with depth and mystery. And let's remember finally that the poet here is seeing something wonderful too, something other than the horses or the blazing stars. The poet is in the place of the parent, watching and marveling at the wonder of a child. It is Lois watching the swallows all over again, it's Lois remembering the swallows, it's me watching her remember her swallows. We can only hope to pass on a love of the world to our children—but moments like the one Coatsworth records in this poem and others, moments where our kids can be open enough to notice new things, moments where the world's energy unexpectedly coalesces into beauty, give us our best chance at succeeding.

When Reaching Is the Rule

Pleasure and Purpose in Gwendolyn Brooks
(2018)

On my refrigerator hangs a sonnet. It was written by my son Rache when he was nine years old (who did not know he was even making a sonnet when he made it), and it opens like this:

Trees do not a forest make,
Through nimble call and barrel quake,
Which makes the oak and pine now shake
To hear these quiet words.

Of course, I realize he was imitating my own sitting down to write sometimes, and there is a pretty heavy influence of Edward Lear in here, but in general, this is a good start to a poem. What I love most about it is that it makes nearly no sense, syntactically or semantically. Or, at least, it is certainly not about the travails of being nine. What it is about is how language sounds. Knowing almost nothing formal about meter and rhyme, his ear gave him a nice mostly tetrameter line and a highly unusual AAAX rhyme scheme. I asked him, in his terms, about the missing foot and the missing rhyme in the last line and he told me he just liked how it sounded. Same goes for the second line which, while metrically predictable, lets "barrel quake" completely undo any standard sense in the poem. It just sounded right, he said, it was fun. And that last comment struck me the most. Making things is fun. Making poems is fun. Making language twist in the ear, slotting words into the pre-drilled holes of form (pre-drilled, of course, so the wood won't crack....), conjuring an almost tangible thing out of the air, is straight-up fun. This, I'm convinced, is what gets the best poets going. It is craft that counts the most.

How rare it seems these days to be told we must read a poet for her or his attention to craft. Instead, we read Dickinson for her proto-feminism, for her avant-avant garde visual compositions. We read Bishop for her wrestling with identity, her cold command over emotion, her loss. We read GM Hopkins for his volcanic encounter with God, William Carlos Williams for his things, Hart Crane for his baroque embraces, Phillis Wheatley for beating back at slavery, John Keats for his doomed youth, John Ashbery for whatever we read Ashbery for, etc. But what all of these poets in my essentially random list were primarily interested in, or at least coevally interested in, was craft—the pleasure of sorting out words in metrical patterns, sonic resonances, strange fellowships. To pretend that Emily Dickinson was more interested in the role of the feminine or the artistic possibilities of the visual than she was in bending common meter and rhyming to her needs is just silly. To imagine that Elizabeth Bishop was not primarily interested in how form, meter and/or rhyme specifically, *makes* poems (even her free-verse poems), is to misread her entirely. Just like my son with his sonnet, good poets aim first for things to sound right. And there is pleasure in that work.

Gwendolyn Brooks is a poet we are often told to read for the way she is situated in the canon—her evocation of Blackness in poetry in a time when there was little other, her not shying away from the difficulties of urban poverty, her radical support of Black arts and her role as a kind of progenitor of Black poetry from the mid twentieth century onward. And these are massively important things. But they are not the only things and can obscure the entirety of this poet. Brooks, beginning her career in the mid-twentieth century, was maybe primarily a formal innovator. Her late work stridently investigates the possibilities of free verse (often the metrical possibilities), and her early work is a sort of masterclass in what meter and rhyme can do to subjects. The ubiquitous "We Real Cool" is as much a poem about how to undo the expectations of dimeter as it is anything else, coming, as it does, in her book *The Bean Eaters* (1960), right after the Blakean toying with rhyme in the title poem. But as I think about Gwendolyn Brooks and the pleasures inherent in making things, I want to look earlier and turn to the beginning sections of her long poem "The Womanhood" from *Annie Allen* (1949).

Here is the beginning of the opening poem of the sequence, a set of sonnets subtitled "The Children of the Poor":

People who have no children can be hard:
Attain a mail of ice and insolence:
Need not pause in the fire, and in no sense
Hesitate in the hurricane to guard.
And when wide world is bitten and bewarred
They perish purely, waving their spirits hence
Without a trace of grace or of offense
To laugh or fail, diffident, wonder-starred.
While through a throttling dark we others hear
The little lifting helplessness, the queer
Whimper-whine; whose unridiculous
Lost softness softly makes a trap for us.
And makes a curse. And makes a sugar of
The malocclusions, the inconditions of love.

Well, that opening line will have you sitting up in your seat for sure. I remember the first time I read this, wondering if I had read it right. And it is not so much, for me, a condemnation of all non-parents as it is a way of setting up the second half of the poem, the lines on the other side of the fulcrum. But before we get there let's look at some of the fabulous things going on in this sonnet. The opening line has a kind of plainness, like the opening of Hopkins's "Spring," which sets up the fireworks that come later in the poem. She employs one of the classic sleight-of-hand tricks of rhyming already in the second line by pre-empting the rhyme sound at the end of "insolence" with the unvoiced "s" in the word "ice." This kind of sudden "double rhyme," if you will, always to my ear has the effect of making the rhyme more surprising, of undoing the potential deadening of a predictable metrical pattern. Also, in this case, it sets up a pattern of alliteration which continues through the whole poem.

Brooks, here and throughout the sequence, delights too in the transformative potential of diction. I'd argue she is under the influence of John Crowe Ransom on this, who was a powerful voice in American poetry still when these poems were written, or at least under the influence of some of the things he set in motion. One can't help but think of his "transmogrifying bee" when we read moments here like "bewarred," "throttling dark," "unridiculous," "malocclusions" or "inconditions." The sudden and surprising diction lifts the reader up out of the familiar and puts us in some other almost clearer place. She is also aware of the way her words sound. In the ninth line, the thick and difficult phrase "throttling dark" is followed in the next line by the soft and musical "little lifting helplessness." This kind of writing is just enchanting to the ear. You can just feel the poet having fun. I could go on and on about this—the unexpected rhyme choices, the clever play with the Italian pattern, the sudden couplets at the end, etc. Suffice to say that form and attention to made details are the heart of this poem. And when we step back from it, when we let the details coalesce into a made whole, we see the beauty and complexity of what is being said.

With such a richly crafted piece, might Brooks also be linking the making of poems to the difficult craft of parenting? I want to consider this as we move through the early part of the sequence. Following my metaphor, the people without children in the first half of the poem, so without these made things, are presented as embodying a kind of crystalline emptiness. An almost inscrutable, nearly lifeless, force. Again, I want to be clear that I am not arguing that this is a fair representation of the childless, and in fact we'd do well to remember the particularities of this speaker—a mother in poverty. But Brooks is certainly also using this tough description to set up the second part of the metaphor, what it means to be buried in the complex mess of making and caring for something other than the self. What I like about this half of the poem is the way it doesn't romanticize child-rearing. In fact, like making poems, it presents the task as essentially impossible. The children are helpless (forever), they are lost (especially in the world of poverty she describes) and their lostness is our trap, which we happily climb into. There is no getting out. And if that is true, if the outcome is either uncertain or certainly doomed, then it is the making, the details of how we write when writing, how we articulate and enact love when loving, that matters.

But wait, you're probably saying at this point. Is there a *craft* in parenting? I suppose it depends how we think of that word. If it means merely a proscribed set of skills being used in historically set patterns (like, say, a weaver's first true go at a basket, or a carpenter's first well-lathed rail), maybe not. But if we mean by craft an attention to something other than the self, or maybe an attention to the self as part of a larger process, not as the full progenitor of the process, we might be on to something. My worst moments as a father come when I lose myself to frustration, to the emotion of the moment. I am much better when some small part of me can perch outside the scene and relay what it sees. For instance, I am known around the house as a kind of clean-up enforcer. I am not proud of this, mind you. But for whatever reason, when I come home from being away at work or wherever I might have gone, I have an instinct to want the house neat, and when it isn't, which with three kids is almost always, I am often described as "raging" around the house picking stuff up and decrying everyone's lack of responsibility. While there may be some small measure of righteousness to my rage, by and large I am out of line in these campaigns. With each mess I come across I get madder and the family gets madder at me. When it is all over, I usually find some time to marvel at how it didn't take that long for me to get it all cleaned up, so it really shouldn't have been a big deal in the first place. However, when I feel those rages coming on, and I manage to send out my little watchman (the poet to my speaker?), who can watch me beginning to rise, I can *see* the scene as a scene. I can see and understand the form of the thing, and how what I am doing is affecting the kids (in my original metaphor, remember, the things being crafted here). Brooks intuits this in the second sonnet of the sequence where she writes "Nor grief nor love shall be enough alone / To ratify my little halves. . . ." Emotion is not enough. We must watch what we are doing as we make choices, and see how those choices affect the whole.

And, oh how I like that phrase "my little halves" in those lines I just quoted. The metaphor suggests at once a division and a wholeness. Our kids, our poems, are at the same time a part of us, and something split off— something we can't entirely control. It is good to keep this in mind. The sonnet sequence, which is just the first part of the larger poem, ends darkly. After a tough sonnet grappling with the inevitability of violence and anger in a young life in poverty, Brooks writes about the death of children. Early death or any death, a death rooted in poverty or any death, the poem, on its largest level, imagines children coping with that ultimate certainty:

When my dears die, the festival-colored brightness
That is their motion and mild repartee

Enchanted, a macabre mockery
Charming the rainbow radiance into tightness
And into a remarkable politeness
That is not kind and does not want to be,
May they not in the crisp encounter see
Something to recognize and read as rightness?
I say they may, so granitely discreet,
The little crooked questionings inbound,
Concede themselves on most familiar ground,
Cold an old predicament of the breath:
Adroit, the shapely prefaces complete,
Accept the university of death.

While it may seem macabre, to borrow Brooks's word, to use a sequence on such tough childhoods to inform my thinking on writing and parenting, she uses the subject to impressive effect as these sonnets conclude. Also, the inherent dissonance between the toughness of the subject and the glittering faceting of the form speaks volumes. This final sonnet functions a bit like the first one except the crucial plain line is in the middle, not the beginning. The sonnet turns in the fifth and sixth line with "a remarkable politeness / That is not kind and does not want to be." The tough acquiescence with which Brooks imagines these children facing death, the "politeness," is perhaps mirrored by the ornate poetics on hand here. If the first sonnet was a slightly altered Italian form, this one is a perfectly regular Italian sonnet. And just as in the first sonnet there are so many wonderful diction moments that pull us out of the poem: "crisp encounter," "granitely discrete," or "little crooked questionings" (mirroring "little lifting helplessness" from the first sonnet). A drumbeat of adjective noun combinations can ruin so much writing, but for Brooks, as she fills out the meter, it seems to offer endless possibilities for widening the reach of the poem. Just taking one of them, "crisp encounter," for instance, we can see her almost completely revising any predictable reading of death. Here death feels like the morning—something fleeting and almost bright, which portends nothing but the start of something new, some new knowledge. Now the speaker is not happy about these deaths, of course, but there is a kind of wise resignation in the final line, that the children are learning, are no longer mere "prefaces" but now becoming full texts themselves, perhaps the very text of this poem. I'm not sure anyone could read this set of poems as *advice* for parents, but it does read as a powerful way of conceptualizing our role as a parent to a child—as a kind of craft, which is made better with specific effort.

. . .

In the garden I am most obsessive in the spring. Before summer takes over, I like neat rows and clean footpaths. I love most, perhaps, the harvest of looking out at the perfect rows and healthy young green plants. When I'm out there, even pulling one weed seems important, even though I know by August it will all be a jungly mess. I'll take the hoe out if I just spot something I missed in a footpath. On the large level, that one weed won't make a difference, and that knowledge would keep me from pulling it. But in the small aesthetic sense, it does matter, and it will affect the way the garden sits in the world. Similarly—when my kids come out to help (which, let's be honest, is rare)—my first impulse is to keep them the hell out of my beautiful garden (!). But the right impulse is instead to include them in the details, to show them how to use the hoe correctly (like a broom, not like an axe), to teach them the difference between lambsquarter and spinach, between cowpeas and pigweed (watch out for thorns!). And then—when the garden becomes more than just aesthetic, when the detail-making starts to pull deeper things into a new and unexpected orbit, the whole enterprise becomes something different, and bigger and more faceted. Just as in poetry, it is always easier to do the plain thing, the prosaic thing, the unadorned thing. But there is a different effect when we reach, when we make things more special by altering a moment with careful attention. If we read Brooks right, our kids' lives, and our lives, are "shapely," are "festival-colored" regardless of the pain they might also hold—so it is up to us to remember that as we move towards our own final knowledge.

Kids, of course, know intuitively to love these details, as my son did in his refrigerator poem. Brooks shifts gears quite suddenly after the hard sonnets, but doesn't give up on her details. The second part of the sequence is a seemingly simple free verse evocation of toddlerhood:

Life for my child is simple, and is good.
He knows his wish. Yes, but that is not all.

Because I know mine too.
And we both want joy of undeep and unabiding things,
Like kicking over a chair or throwing blocks out of a window
Or tipping over an ice box pan
Or snatching down curtains or fingering an electric outlet
Or a journey or a friend or an illegal kiss.
No. There is more to it than that.
It is that he has never been afraid.
Rather, he reaches out and lo the chair falls with a beautiful crash,
And the blocks fall, down on the people's heads,
And the water comes slooshing sloppily out across the floor.
And so forth.
Not that success, for him, is sure, infallible.
But never has he been afraid to reach.
His lesions are legion.
But reaching is his rule.

There is a lot for us to learn from here. First off, despite the disarmingly plain first line, the poem isn't simple. While it is something of a break formally from the tighter sonnets, you can see how she ties this free verse poem into the earlier pieces. The first line of the poem is a perfect line of pentameter (with a pronounced trochee in the first foot, giving us a big stress on the word "life," when the stressed word we ended the sonnet sequence on was, of course, "death."). The poem then retains an iambic character in its uneven lines, while touching base with pentameter itself often enough to keep it in our ear: the tenth line is a perfect pentameter and also a sentence on its own, tacking itself forcefully onto the fabric of the poem, and the third to last line and then the last two lines put together, are gestures of pentameter, with two stretching anapests to start things off in those final lines. How interesting that in this poem written in free verse, the more "innovative" style of the time, the poet emphasizes the child's reaching, his ambition and thirst for more, in a final pentameter. In early Brooks, as in Bishop, innovation saw the poet understanding craft in all of its contexts, never jettisoning anything, but seeking meaning in her moves instead.

It feels to me no accident, either, that in this poem of playful metrical exuberance, we have the line, "And we both want joy of undeep and unabiding things." As Brooks connects her playing with language to the toddler's playing with the new things of the world, we start to understand what makes those "undeep" things so important. Maybe we can only access the deep by remembering the pleasures of play. In overturning the things of his world, the toddler will encounter real pain and real joy. So too the poet. It is when we fixate on finding pain and joy as we write poems, if I follow Brooks here, that we tend to miss it. Frost, who Brooks admired, insists, in an essay on E.A. Robinson, that "The play's the thing. Play's the thing." And here in Brooks's beautiful sequence she echoes that sentiment and ties it directly to our engagement with childhood, whether as parents or our past lives as children ourselves. And by the end of the poem Brooks connects this idea of undeepness, of reaching and playing, to the idea of failure. Frost, in that same essay, writes of Robinson, "His theme was unhappiness itself, but his skill was as happy as it was playful." It is a crucial recognition that we can't always salvage joy, but we can make its loss more meaningful through efforts at beauty, and, pointedly, at fun. That last point seems crucial for Brooks here. In this extremely tough sequence—one which touches on poverty, on slavery, on racism, on class—she refuses ever to stop playing with language, to give up on the beauty of the gesture, on the act of expressiveness.

As parents, maybe this is our takeaway. We can't overlook the significance of the *act* of parenting. The little gestures that make up our children's childhoods—the hurried ham sandwich we slap down in front of our kids, the rustling up out of bed, the oscillating fan slowly turning in a too hot upstairs room, the stuffed animal we bring in wet from a rainy morning, the dogs we tend, the rooster crowing while we fill bowls with blackberries, the stories read at bedtime, the first time they brush their hair, the last time they want us to wash their hair, the movies they love, the chores they hate—these things are part of that craft I was guessing at earlier. We can recognize our movements in this form, Brooks seems to be saying, and work with the wild ambition of the child. As an analogy, if the heart of a poem is its energy, and form is its container, then the child and the acts of a parent might be on the other side of that double colon. And we do these things knowing that we will fail. It's a bit too like faith. You can't have true faith unless you are sure you will doubt and fail that very faith many times. Complexity demands failure. As such, and happily, failure can be no real deterrent. We keep making dinners, keep explaining morals, keep clearing stains, *anyway*. And when we can remember to make our gestures with a clear head, thinking of these larger contexts, focusing on the details of the gesture alongside the larger meanings, I think we do a better job of it.

• • •

Fittingly, the next poem in the sequence, and the last I'll discuss, is one seemingly of pure play. I mentioned John Crowe Ransom earlier, and this poem, "the ballad of the light-eyed little girl," reads almost like a mash-up of "Bells for John Whiteside's Daughter" and "Janet Waking," two of his more famous poems, and ones that Brooks certainly would have known. What Brooks would have admired about Ransom in those two poems is his evocation of the pain of death within the joys and wild strivings of childhood (beginning to sound familiar?). Also, there is an interesting kinship between Ransom's southern world and the world of urban Chicago that Brooks creates (and there is an irony of there, of course, of which I am aware). Of course, Ransom's world is sometimes a bit genteel for a straight semblance; a better comparison might be to Brooks's direct contemporary, George Scarbrough (perhaps the most undervalued poet of this generation), who we've discussed and whose poetics and evocations of a poor Appalachian sharecropping community have many ties to Brooks's concerns. Anyhow, her poem opens:

Sweet Sally took a cardboard box
And in went pigeon poor.
Whom she had starved to death but not
For lack of love be sure.

The wind it harped as twenty men.
The wind it harped like hate.
It whipped our light-eyed girl,
It made her wince and wait.

The playfulness of the (mostly) hymn meter here is in direct contrast to the weightier gesture of pentameter at the end of the previous poem. Moreover, the strict formal construction contrasts with the intermittent free verse in that poem. And the rhyming here is song-like. It is not baroque, or obscured by enjambment as in the sonnets, but it is on full and unapologetic display. Later in the poem Sally buries the pigeon (more than poor Chucky gets in Ransom's poem):

She has taken her passive pigeon poor,
She has buried him down and down.
He never shall sally to Sally
Nor soil any roofs of the town.

This is just straight-up fun. Not only can Brooks not resist the pun on Sally's name (and the fun of the deliberate and rhyming archaism of "shall"), but she manages, as does Ransom in "Bells for John Whiteside's Daughter" to work some childishly delightful bird poop into the poem. And it is her pleasure in simply writing that makes this poem work in the sequence. What some might dismiss as silly, as a surface gesture (honestly, who would attempt this poem now?), instead fits into this tough sequence of poems as a gesture of childhood itself. The poem ends with a small funeral:

She has sprinkled nail polish on dead dandelions
And children have gathered around
Funeral for him whose epitaph
Is "PIGEON—Under the ground."

The poem somehow at once acknowledges the failed reachings of the child, while also acknowledging the realness of death. It suddenly, with all its playful gestures of form and diction, becomes quite serious. It is most like Ransom's "Janet Waking," in this regard, but it is best, of course, set next to the other poems by Brooks I've discussed here. If the sonnets were the perspective of a third person mother (the mother of the poor), and the second poem was the perspective of the poet mother, then this poem gives us the world as seen by the child. The same lesson writ small, or seemingly small I suppose.

So what are we left with? Play for play's sake? Play for the chance something big might happen? I think all of these. But the big things, I'll argue finally, aren't what bring the poet back to the desk or the parent back to the sandwich, or the gardener back to the dirt. My son isn't writing poems because he thinks he might finally get the pain of existence exactly right. He writes because it is fun, and those other things will perhaps one day follow. The same process is true for a formal master like the early Brooks I've considered here. What keeps the opening poems of this sequence moving is the pleasure of language—the many formal gestures and fireworks of diction that pulse through the lines. And, of course, the reaching for these effects, the pleasure and play in the language become part of, or most of, the meaning of the poem as well.

To describe parenthood or poverty or pain in the terms of playfulness and language-pleasure, changes the way we understand such things. It evokes them with a complexity and humanity that wouldn't quite be there another way. Good poems, like all children, share such complexity, a complexity made of the tension between the gestures we can control and the deep currents we can't. Probably, our failures on both fronts come when we forget this—when we think it is the deep currents that we control, and not the small gestures of detail, we end up forgetting how the whole process works and make a mockery of it instead. The Scottish poet Edwin Muir asserts, in discussing this very problem, that "deliberate intention" will always end up distracting the poet, that, instead and by contrast, a song "that sings for its own pleasure will give back to us for centuries the emotion out of which it was born." As parents and as poets, we can't control the deep lesions or the sudden joys, to go back to Brooks, but we can face with pleasure, and for their inherent pleasure, the small tasks and the great reaches before us and maybe make something that will last.

Keeping the Door Unlocked

Darkness in Frost
(2019)

Where we live, off a road off a road eleven miles from a small town in central Virginia, it gets dark. Having grown up just north of Atlanta, and having lived in densely populated places as a young adult, this was a new phenomenon for me when we moved here. In fact, and if you've spent time in rural places maybe you'll understand this, it is so dark outside that on some nights you don't really need a light to get around. I can go shut the chicken coop, if I've forgotten, in the complete darkness but can see enough to get myself there. In fact, on the occasions that I bring a lantern, if one of the dogs is with me or if I need to count the hens, it is a bit harder to see. There's been a lot of talk in the last few years about light pollution and the best way to see stars—and that, of course, is important (I would have trouble overstating how much the milky way is a constant and beloved companion for our family), but I am interested here in the darkness as a presence even down on the ground—not just when we're looking to the heavens, though we'll have some of that too.

Earlier this summer (it's July now), I took the kids outside around 9:00—they were headed to bed—to watch the fireflies (or lightning bugs, depending on where you grew up). The insects had really just emerged, and they were booming—patchworking the trees with pinpoint light, like string-bulbs strewn by a manic decorator working behind schedule. It was mesmerizing. Of course we were there to see the lightning bugs, but it was the darkness that made it possible. The dark, for these insects, is literally the medium of their communication, and for us watchers it was the medium of our awe. The kids stared raptly at the eruption of greeny flares in the trees for a few minutes and then decided they were a little scared of being outside so far from the house in the dark, and they turned and half-ran to bed. And the way that ended should remind me here that I'm not trying to romanticize darkness. I mean I could stuff your ears and eyes with maple syrup writing about kids and fireflies, but those kinds of anecdotes overlook the reality of the thing. There is beauty and fear in the image. There is the known and the unknown—and for kids, and really for all of us, the unknown is at once sort of thrilling and sort of terrifying.

The poet who, for me, most effectively wrestles with the darkness—and his is a country darkness too—is Robert Frost. I've been reading Frost for as long as I've been interested in poetry, and his alternately mystical and skeptical relationship with the natural world, its light and its darkness, has always seemed to me one of the most complex iterations of what it means to be human in all of American literature. I could write here about any number of Frost's famous poems—the ambivalent dreamscape of "After Apple-Picking," the discursive philosophy of "Birches," the sardonic insight of "The Road Not Taken"—but I'll try to work with some slightly less familiar examples of Frost's digging down into the darkness around him.

Here's the last poem of his second book, *North of Boston* (1914), the first of his books, actually, to be published in the US:

GOOD HOURS

I had for my winter evening walk—
No one at all with whom to talk,
But I had the cottages in a row
Up to their shining eyes in snow.

And I thought I had the folk within:
I had the sound of a violin;
I had a glimpse through curtain laces
Of youthful forms and youthful faces.

I had such company outward bound.
I went till there were no cottages found.
I turned and repented, but coming back
I saw no window but that was black.

Over the snow my creaking feet
Disturbed the slumbering village street
Like profanation, by your leave,
At ten o'clock of a winter eve.

This is one of those poems that glitters more the more you read it. It is deceptively simple—reading a bit like a draft of his famous later poem, "Acquainted with the Night." But, really, the poems couldn't be more different. That poem is locked in the speaker's head—the only human sounds are far away—whereas in this poem the speaker feels and connects with the human world all through the poem. It opens with a kind of declaration of what should be loneliness undone by the conjunction "but." It is almost cheerful in the way it imagines the fullness of his company, a company that is figured from the outset by light—the "shining eyes" of the houses that watch the walker on his route. The second quatrain then moves inside these friendly houses and is full of sound and bustle, a community the speaker feels embraced by.

The poem breaks in half here, as do most walks, and turns to silence and darkness. Those light-filled windows are now, quite simply, "black." A simplistic version of this poem would merely relate the sadness of this emptiness, but Frost is too cagey for that. In fact, he knows we will be trying to read the poem that way, and so surprises us in the final stanza, when we, the readers, are implicated. That marvelous "by your leave," suggests that the poet/walker is not alone after all—we've been with him all along. And that "profanation," the half-mocking simile in the penultimate line which connects to the jokey use of the verb "repent" in the previous stanza, feels almost like what he is profaning was our preconceived idea of where this poem was going to go. It doesn't go there—the speaker is not scared or sad in the darkness of the town. Instead, he is simply walking still, in the embrace of the "good hours" from the title—those that are filled with light *and* those filled with darkness.

• • •

So if the darkness isn't always scary, and it also isn't always nourishing, what is it? As parents, we are often shielding our kids from things. In fact, parents have gotten so good at protecting their kids that some are getting a bad rap for it. A lot of parents of my generation spend time lamenting the disappearance of what they perceive as the freedom of our 1980s childhoods. What I think a lot of people forget is that our parents had a much clearer idea of where we were than we remember (we were kids after all, how reliable are our memories?), and places were much less crowded than they are now. Case in point: the street I grew up on outside of Atlanta would often go half an hour without a car on it when I was a kid. It now goes rarely half a minute. How might that change where a kid should go on her bike? So when I'm talking about darkness here, I'm not talking about danger. We should shield our kids from danger at every opportunity. However, we cannot shield them from the presence of danger. In this distinction, maybe, is the difference. We don't abandon our kids to darkness, but, instead, teach them that it is there and how to navigate it.

So what might this look like in practice? Here's a small example: A little more than a year ago our neighbor's wife died. She had been sick a long while, but her death was still a surprise. There was a funeral and gathering at our neighbor's house one Saturday—it was hot and there was barbecue and tea and no small amount of sadness. One bright spot, however, was a group of puppies that were milling around the food, one of whom was named Meatball. Lois, our youngest, played with Meatball the whole time, and in fact designated herself the official protector of the food against Meatball's sorties. He was a small black puppy, somewhere between a beagle and a lab, full of energy and brightness. I knew Lee was planning on keeping Meatball, and so a few weeks after the funeral he stopped his tractor to chat for a bit and I asked after the dog, remembering how much Lois had enjoyed playing with it. He told me sadly that Meatball, and all his litter mates, had died around the same time—most likely parvo or something along those lines.

The compounded loss of the puppy on top of the recent funeral was hard for me to wrap my head around and even harder when a few days later Lois happened to ask me about Lee and Meatball. I was frozen for a moment, at once realizing that I had deliberately not said anything about it to her and now wondering what I should do in the moment. Do I tell her? She was only six after all. Do I lie? How dark is the truth?

I'm pretty sure I weaseled out of telling her the first time, to my discredit—but eventually I had to come clean. She looked at me matter-of-factly and said that it was sad. I agreed. When, a few months later, Lee got a new coonhound puppy named Abe, Lois seemed especially happy for him. So it turns out, I guess, that for kids (and the rest of us) the truth is dark, but it is a darkness that we have to be comfortable in or at least one we can look in the eye.

Here's another poem by Frost, from his book *New Hampshire*:

EVENING IN A SUGAR ORCHARD

From where I lingered in a lull in March
Outside the sugar-house one night for choice,
I called the fireman with a careful voice
And bade him leave the pan and stoke the arch:
'O fireman, give the fire another stoke,
And send more sparks up chimney with the smoke.'
I thought a few might tangle, as they did,
Among bare maple boughs, and in the rare
Hill atmosphere not cease to glow,
And so be added to the moon up there.
The moon, though slight, was moon enough to show
On every tree a bucket with a lid,
And on black ground a bear-skin rug of snow.
The sparks made no attempt to be the moon.
They were content to figure in the trees
As Leo, Orion, and the Pleiades.
And that was what the boughs were full of soon.

I've always admired this poem, though, again, it is not one of Frost's traditional greatest hits. I love the way it is both elemental and human—the "fireman" seeming every bit some kind of combination of Prometheus or the devil (one thinks in this poem of the blacksmith from *Moby-Dick* as well), while the syrup operation itself feels very human and of the world of commerce and daily concerns. And in fact this dualism in the poem seems bound entirely into the poem's central image—the sparks of industry become (or "figure" as) the constellations in the sky, which finish as a kind of fiery celestial fruit in the branches of the trees. So, to follow, the sparks are earthly, then heavenly, then brought, still with the sheen of heaven on them, back to earth. This is the same sort of narrative we see in the final section of the more famous "Birches," but in this poem it is the dark backdrop of the night sky that makes the image sing.

So many things in this poem suggest the sense of darkness I was trying to pin down earlier. In the second line, the speaker of the poem points out that he has stopped "one night for choice,"—so this is no terrified night traveler. He enjoys the darkness, and even by the sugar house, with its warm glow of work, he'd rather stay outside with the stars. He even suggests, tongue in cheek as ever with Frost, that there is something magic going on; the "rare / Hill atmosphere" has a supernatural effect on the sparks and freezes them in place. Of course this is just Frost doing an ancient human thing—telling stories to explain natural phenomena. But in his hands, in this poem of labor and human doings, it also becomes a poem about not forgetting the magic of the unknown. That to give yourself over to the night, to mystery, with its fires and shadows, is as crucial a part of being human as any industrious work. That the two, really, must go hand in hand. Note how the syrup worker, the "fireman," accedes to the request of the speaker. He too, in the poem, is a willing aesthete, and he recognizes, even without saying it, that the beauty of the sparks in the new-evening sky is as important a product as the syrup being made from the sap surrounding them both in buckets hanging like strange knobby branches from the trees.

There is a clear connection, in considering this poem, to the lightning bugs we started with—though none of them hung on long enough to become stars as far as I could tell—but there are also connections to the tougher darknesses we've been hunting here. There's a strange melancholy surrounding the moon in the second half of the poem. The moon is "slight" but "moon enough" to do its work. But even with that, the sparks can't aspire to the moon's great light. "The sparks made no attempt to be the moon," Frost writes in the fourteenth line, underlining perhaps the limitations of the magic and the light. The dark is still going to win out in a way, but the sparks can work within it. Even the moon in the poem is not enough to dispel the deepening shadows of the coming night. It is just enough to let us see a little. And somewhere between pure darkness and pure light is the truth, is the way we make our way in the world. At Bonnie's funeral there was a joyful puppy; light and dark. The puppy died;

I lied; a new dog arrived. Sadness and change, all of it full of some sort of light and some sort of darkness. To pretend otherwise, to ourselves or to our kids, seems foolish.

And speaking of that new dog, the coon hound,—he's now fully grown into an endearing neighborly nuisance. He's discovered the wild fun to be had with our younger dog, Cinnamon, who is a sixty-pound yellow mutt, and now comes to the door like a gentleman caller almost every day. We watch them play—running huge circles around the grapes and the flowers, chewing on each other's ears. He is so determined to come and play that most times I have to either call Lee to come get him or I have to take him back over there myself, usually with one or all of the kids in tow. Yesterday Lois walked him back with me, and Abe held her hand in his mouth the entire walk back, they looked like old friends out for a stroll holding hands. When we get to Lee's, or he comes by to pick Abe up, he always seems just as happy to see us as he is frustrated that Abe keeps getting away. It is good, perhaps, to have reasons for neighbors to see one another. When I take Abe and put him back in his pen, we can hear his joyful coonhound seal howl still sounding through the meadow and woods even when we get back to our house.

• • •

Here's another story, this one about birds. Two years ago we trimmed our butterfly bush. I bought the plant many years ago from our friend Eli, who has since closed his magical greenhouse and moved away. Like a fool, I put it in the flower garden, not knowing that it would eventually be over ten feet tall and nearly as wide. Not exactly a good match for the baptisia, balloon flowers and other blooming things we have in there. So the fall after I misplanted it, I moved it to a spot in front of the big room, on the north end of our house. I wasn't sure the plant would survive the transplant, but I bought a second one to keep it company and encourage it along. It did survive and the two butterfly bushes are now an enormous fixture of summer here—their coral-purple columns of flowers filling the air around our house with monarchs, swallowtails, morphos, humming-birds and countless other winged things.

But back to the trimming—they hadn't bloomed very well the year before, so Kate pruned the bushes pretty hard in the spring and found a cardinal's nest. We knew it was cardinals because the female bird was barking at us as we looked inside and saw a small clutch of speckled eggs. We kept close tabs on the nest, leaving the branches around it for protection, and looking in on the eggs whenever we thought the parents weren't around. In a few days, the eggs hatched and I held Lois up to see over the edge of the nest where three or four feathery marbles with beaks were mewling and figuring out how to open their eyes. In another day or so they were cheeping and taking food from the parents; we could see the flames of red and gray from the big room window as both birds collected insects for the opening mouths.

Soon after, the nest was empty. The birds were certainly not big enough to fly away, so something must have taken the babies, and we never saw the older birds again. The suddenness of this small emptiness was hard even for me to grasp, much less the kids. Lois asked me to hoist her up to the nest to see what I could already see. I hesitated (as with Meatball), but told her what I saw and showed her. All of us gathered around, then, to stare at the little grail of straw and chaff that waved empty in the branches of the butterfly bush and thought about the tides of loss that organize the world. This summer, the cardinals moved to the nandina directly in front of the big room window. We could see into the nest even from inside the house, and this time the eggs never even hatched. One day they were there, like little chocolates in a perfect palm, and the next day they were gone—secreted, most likely, in a black snake's long belly.

Here's Frost on this situation, but in reverse:

THE NEED OF BEING VERSED IN COUNTRY THINGS

The house had gone to bring again
To the midnight sky a sunset glow.
Now the chimney was all of the house that stood,
Like a pistil after the petals go.

The barn opposed across the way,
That would have joined the house in flame
Had it been the will of the wind, was left
To bear forsaken the place's name.

No more it opened with all one end
For teams that came by the stony road
To drum on the floor with scurrying hoofs
And brush the mow with the summer load.

The birds that came to it through the air
At broken windows flew out and in,
Their murmur more like the sigh we sigh
From too much dwelling on what has been.

Yet for them the lilac renewed its leaf,
And the aged elm, though touched with fire;
And the dry pump flung up an awkward arm;
And the fence post carried a strand of wire.

For them there was really nothing sad.
But though they rejoiced in the nest they kept,
One had to be versed in country things
Not to believe the phoebes wept.

In this poem it is the humans who have disappeared with birds left in their wake. But the poem wrestles with the same strange sense of inevitable loss and cyclical return that is bound up in my stories of the cardinals and the cardinal eggs. I always marvel how beautiful, in Frost's hands, the ruins here become. The house "had gone" to make way for the fire's sunset, and the chimney is the center of a once prime flower. Here, graciously for this poet, the human world is one with the natural world—it shares in its presence and in its beauty. But, for that, it also has to share in the cruel impassivity of natural things—the "will of the wind" in the second stanza feeling like some kind of Old Testament force of destruction.[1]

Only once in the poem does Frost allow himself to be nostalgic—in the third stanza where he imagines the busy work of the barn. That is quickly done away with by the half-humorous simile in the next stanza,

---

1. The "will of the wind" also recalls the title of Frost's first book, *A Boy's Will*, which, in turn, takes its name from Longfellow's poem "My Lost Youth," whose famous chorus is "A boy's will is the wind's will"—so the human and the natural are really bound up tight here.

the bird's murmuring "like the sigh we sigh / From too much dwelling on what has been." So what is Frost saying to us here? That we shouldn't mourn? That we shouldn't let the sadnesses of the past inform or pollute the potential joys of the future? I'm not sure. I think he's saying that it is inevitable that they will, and that we have to make hay anyway.

Of course the crucial part of the poem is the last two stanzas, where the poet turns to the titular "country things" (note the pun on the word "versed" here) in order to avoid saying the unsayable—a word for the nuanced combination of loss and life that he is getting at in the poem. He seats it here in the birds—the phoebes, which are reveling in the emergence of spring, the turning of the always-turning year. They are, in the poem, both happy and sad. Though they are "rejoicing," we, the unversed observer, hear them as mourning. What Frost accomplishes in that moment is the negative capability of loss. That we lose and we love, all at the same time—they are inseparable from one another. In fact, the birds (and phoebes are small birds, who build small nests) have likely built their nest literally in and on the ruins of this old house—so their joy is propped up by these signifiers of loss. Who knows but if every time I bring a bird's nest that I found on the ground inside—where the kids marvel at it and insist on putting it on display—it too hasn't been the site of loss? We know that animals mourn—so how would the cardinals see us? How do we see ourselves?

This poem reminds us that, at once, we cannot allow ourselves unending mourning, and we can't expect the world to mourn with us. What we can do, though, is recognize that sometimes what looks like indifference—the relentless turning year, the churning of the moon through the calendar—can also be a site of joy. Because we must carry on, we do.

. . .

I started this essay with fear, and I'm going to end there too. But this time a fear we have to engage in a different way. While I was working on this essay, the country suffered yet another bout of random gun violence—on streets in Chicago, in a Walmart in El Paso, TX, and outside a bar in Dayton, OH. It seems that nowhere we go is completely safe from guns any longer. Kids are legitimately scared to go to school, parents are buying bulletproof backpack inserts, and few new laws are being passed. What do we do with this fear? Is this a darkness we have to live with? I'm going to say yes and no. The opaque force at the heart of these things is not something that will ever go away. Whether we believe these events are inspired and/or tangentially encouraged by insidious political rhetoric, widening cultural chasms, a fevered and ungrammatical distortion of the meaning of the Second Amendment, and growing ignorance of our own history, or whether we believe that poor mental health care is chiefly to blame (and why are these things considered separate concerns?), there are tangible things we can do to make the darkness less dark. Never in any of his poems does Frost argue for giving in to darkness—he just argues that it is there.

And maybe it's the elemental nature of the darkness I've been considering here that we can use to think about the violence all around us. I hear a lot about how there is nothing we can really do about gun violence— that there are already too many guns for any restrictions to help, that an assault weapons ban would only encourage people to own them, etc. But is nothing really the only alternative? Think what an example we are setting for our kids. This week I have had two large sweetgum trees near the house cut down. They have shed wood out of their crowns for years, and I am always scared whenever there is a big storm. Will my cutting them keep any other tree from falling? No. Is it some palpable measure of more safety? Yes. I can't stop the wind from blowing, but I can take some of its tools. Why can't we do the same with the winds of gun violence? We absolutely cannot stop the entirety of such darkness—but we can do something (stronger background checks, mandatory gun insurance, registration fees, bans and restrictions on any weapon not built for hunting animals, etc.). We can acknowledge the shadow that it casts and move more surely within it.

Here's Frost one more time:

THE LOCKLESS DOOR

It went many years,
But at last came a knock,
And I thought of the door
With no lock to lock.

I blew out the light,
I tip-toed the floor,
And raised both hands
In prayer to the door.

But the knock came again.
My window was wide;
I climbed on the sill
And descended outside.

Back over the sill
I bade a 'Come in'
To whatever the knock
At the door may have been.

So at a knock
I emptied my cage
To hide in the world
And alter with age.

This poem comes right before "The Need of Being Versed in Country Things," and is an interesting counterweight to it. In that poem, all the action is in the natural world—its movement apart from us and its balancing of loss and happiness. This poem happens only in the human world—in the dark retreats of the psyche. What I love about this poem is its ineffable strangeness—the speaker feels trapped in the first few stanzas of the poem—trapped by his own fear of the unknown. But when that fear comes to fruition—he is saved not by ignoring it, or refusing to open the door, but by action. By at once inviting the feared thing into the room ("whatever the knock / At the door may have been") and leaving the room, he both recognizes the reality of the darkness's presence, but also refuses to be cowed by it, refuses even to lock the door. I love the way we can't *quite* make out the meaning in the last stanza—"I emptied my cage / To hide in the world." So is he the knocker as well? What is the cage—the room or his mind? And then that final line—that in growing, our relationship with the darkness, the fears all around us, will change. So how do we help our kids negotiate these things? We tell them the world is not a waiting game—but nor is it a game that we can outright win. Living is simply a game that we have to play—with all of its arcane rules, its cheats and its prizes.

The tree service hasn't come back to clean up one of the gums they brought down, so sections of its trunk are spaced across the driveway like logrolling logs in one of those lumberjack competitions that used to be on TV when I was a kid, or like some strange archipelago of cigar shaped islands. The kids are having a blast leaping from the stump to the first log to the next log and all the way to the end of the island chain. They leapt and jumped deep into the August evening last night, to where they could barely see. Jane Bell especially seemed to get a thrill as the logs shifted slightly under her weight when she landed. She only fell once, navigating this tree that could easily have fallen on the house in the next storm. I hate to cut things down. And even though I did it to keep her safe—she's finding good ways to keep things dangerous, in the growing dark, all the same.

Already Wide Enough

Edwin Arlington Robinson and the Lives of Others
(2019)

My son Rache, who is now a few months past eleven, has picked up a few
privileges of late. For instance, he can now, with a helmet, ride his bike
down to the road, around by the mailbox on to our neighbor Lee's house,
down the field road and back into our yard. This is probably a three-
quarter mile loop, so he's well outside of my sight and hearing when he's
gone. While I, of course, remember cycling to what seemed like destina-
tions on other planets in my eighties and nineties childhood, having him
off on his own was still a step for his mom and me. Also, out here in the
country while cars are relatively few and far between, those that do come
by come by fast, and they aren't expecting kids on bicycles, so there is
legitimate cause for caution.

But he's thrilled with his sense of freedom. While there is technically
nowhere to "go" out here (unlike in my childhood suburban bike-scape),
he loves just the open sense of possibility as he rides—the fact of himself
in motion. And alone. And maybe that's the crucial part of it. He is with
himself out there, and, for now, that is an exhilarating feeling. When he
returns from a loop (his term), he is usually out of breath, his long hair
helmet-shaped and half sweat-stuck to his face, he often has some small
story—he waved at Lee, or he passed the Amish family on their buggy, or
he passed one of the Amish children in their miniature buggy (hooked
to Starburst, the miniature pony), or Lee's dog Abe chased him down the
road, tongue as long as his ears, or he saw a feral kitten that might need
rescuing, etc. And when he tells me these stories, I'm always struck by
how he is beginning to limn out what life looks like from a singular perspective. Does that make sense? What I mean is that he is beginning to

understand that he is stuck inside himself. When he cycled off that first time, beyond our eyes, Kate and I could feel physically the space between him and us increase. Or it made itself increasingly perceptible. Now he is beginning to understand that that space is a permanent feature of living, and that that can be a thing that is scary, and a thing to be celebrated.

When I think of the spaces between people, one poet comes to mind immediately: Edwin Arlington Robinson. Now, I have written about this space in thinking about Elizabeth Bishop—but with Bishop, she more often spends time imagining the space, whereas Robinson, one might say, expends his energy in imagining the person on the other side. Robinson is probably one of the most underappreciated American poets of the twentieth century. In ways, he should also be noted as one of our great dramatists and novelists—not because he wrote extensively in those forms, but because his poetry at its best is always imagining the lives of others. We generally come to Robinson, if we come to him, through some of his early Tilbury Town poems—poems like "Miniver Cheevy" or "Richard Cory" or "Mr. Flood's Party"—each small masterpieces of finding the empty spaces in, and stretched out before, other's lives. And while his poems are almost relentlessly dark, we can read him as also pointing ways towards, if not light, a safer spot in the darkness.

When you imagine the life of another person—whether it be in fiction or in reality—you are practicing empathy. In our visual world, we are often briefly asked to consider others through photographs—migrants dead in the rushes in the Rio Grande, an Afghan girl's haunted eyes, a poignant selfie. But this kind of empathy through immediacy strikes me as something other than what Robinson is up to. An image does not always allow us a deep dive into the complexities of the other life, it is instead a kind of blunt summary, so blunt we almost bounce off of it right back to ourselves. What Robinson reminds us in his poems is that empathy, true empathy, is hard. And it's hard because we are naturally selfish. We are of the self, trapped inside. It is hard work, maybe impossible work, for me to try to conceive of Rache's experience on that bike—what he sees and how it makes him feel, what the slow hills here mean to him inside *his* skin, if he notices the paler yellow of July's roadside weeds, if he wonders how Lee is managing now on his own. Robinson not only sings of this distance, this impossible space between us, but he also tries to find ways to cross it and get to the person on the other side. Can I do the same?

Let's start with a small sad sonnet from Robinson's 1920 book *The Three Taverns*. I have a small brown first edition of this book, which I cherish, and which is even dedicated to some possible distant relatives of mine with whom Robinson was close friends. It is one of the few books that I will just carry around with me in my bag should I find myself, say, waiting on an oil change or on a plane. It doesn't have any of the famous Tilbury Town poems in it, but something about its mood—the devastating sadness of "The Mill," the Modern weirdness of its masterpiece, "Tasker Norcross"—always amazes me. But let's start with the sonnet I mentioned, "A Song at Shannon's." Here's the poem:

A SONG AT SHANNON'S

Two men came out of Shannon's, having known
The faces of each other for so long
As they had listened there to an old song,
Sung thinly in a wastrel monotone
By some unhappy night-bird, who had flown
Too many times and with a wing too strong
To save himself; and so done heavy wrong
To more frail elements than his alone.

Slowly away they went, leaving behind
More light than was before them. Neither met
The other's eyes again or said a word.
Each to his loneliness or to his kind,
Went his own way, and with his own regret,
Not knowing what the other may have heard.

I guess I read this poem as both an elegy and a warning. It is an elegy for what might have been—two lonelinesses (to steal Robinson's word) assuaged by companionship—and a warning against what is more common, leaving each other alone. I love the line breaks in this poem. The first line hanging on that abstract idea of "having known"—having known what? Their fate? The fact of their aloneness? And then when the second line resumes the clause, we learn of the relationship between the two men as fellow patrons of the bar. But then we also learn that another thing they both knew was the song of the bird who takes over the rest of the opening octet. The bird is clearly supposed to be symbolic of the men, but it also suggests the thing between them, the space they haven't breached, the space they maybe haven't even acknowledged (and that space sings!).

The sestet leaves the bird behind (though it is perched still in our minds), and we have a fabulous and classically Robinsonian moment—where the poet literally describes the scene: as these two men move into the darkness of the street, they are leaving the warm light of the pub behind them. But of course it is instantly metaphorical as well—it is the light of companionship, of closeness and of the known and familiar that they are leaving behind. They are entering the darkness of their loneliness, the usual unknown of the outside world. I am also always struck by the inclusion of the phrase "or to his kind" in the fourth line of the sestet. Robinson needed the rhyme, of course, but it adds weight and nuance to the idea of loneliness here. It suggests that these men aren't necessarily alone all the time but surrounded by like-minded people—family maybe—but in Robinson's turn of phrase it sounds more like our idea of a bubble. When we are surrounded only by people who share our opinions, who think like us, our empathic skills are often not challenged, and our "companionships" can be as much echo chambers as anything else, leaving us, in ways, more alone. I think that is what Robinson is getting at. These two men held something new for each other—an opportunity to try to see the world through another's loneliness, to cross the space between them instead of pretending it is not there or merely using it as a mirror.

This reading seems to be bolstered by the final two lines. Both men have an ambiguous regret, and both are locked so deeply in themselves it hasn't occurred to either that the song (from the opening lines) may have sounded differently to different ears, that the world is not the world seen only through our one pair of eyes. When Rache goes off on his bike to see our little local world, he sees different things than I do. When he tells me about what he sees it enlarges my idea of this place, and of him, and in turn of myself in this place and with him. When we don't recognize that space between each other, and then each other across it, Robinson ultimately warns us, we are left again on the cold road alone.

• • •

Robinson himself commented on this penchant for suggesting joy's, or love's, absence in his poems—that a focus on that absence in itself (by negation) could make joy a subject. He once wrote to a friend that his poems were "written with a conscious hope that they might make some despairing devil a little stronger." Later in the letter he complains that readers (or reviewers especially) don't see any happiness in his poems because he doesn't "dance on [an] illuminated hilltop and sing about the bobolinks and bumble-bees."[1] In Robinson's view, true uplift comes from acknowledging the vast gulfs of darkness any human being must negotiate. When we ignore them with a forced smile, he seems to be saying, we risk misunderstanding, or not perceiving, the complexity of joy.

Now all of this is a hard thing to get across to an eleven-year old, so I'm wondering if you've maybe been rolling your eyes a little, but you'll have to hang with me. I'm not arguing that I need to explain Robinson's darkness to Rache, but that I need to keep in mind his warnings when I am thinking about how best to parent this boy who is nearly not a boy anymore. Adolescence itself, as you may remember, can seem pretty dark. But I'm going to contend here that it is not the age that is dark, though a lot of commentary on social media would have you think otherwise, but just being human. Adolescence is when we first become aware of our humanity and aware of how that is not always a pretty thing to see.

In addition to riding his bike further abroad, Rache is also using his ears a bit more—he listens to everything: everything Kate and I say to each other, everything the radio says, all the lyrics to songs, etc. And he has a lot of questions, especially anytime he hears something that involves the word "war" or "bombs" or "mass shooting" or a story about missing kids (or kids separated from their parents at the border). We are constantly having to explain what the news was actually about, or calm him down about what the news was actually about. What he is doing, of course, is attempting to align what he hears about the world with what he knows about his own small world. I guess we all do this in a way, but it

1. From an 1897 letter to Harry Smith, quoted in Scott Donaldson's wonderful biography of Robinson (pg. 123)

is a crucial moment in a young life—to try to make a move toward empathy instead of just panicked guardedness. What I want him to know more than anything is that those scary things, those things we can't control, do not exist in opposition to the joys we have, the small close comforts of beauty and warmth and safety. But they instead exist alongside them, are entangled with them. Grasping the coeval nature of pain and security takes a lifetime of effort, and he's just starting out!

Before I turn to some of Robinson's longer poems, let's look at a small verse on this subject:

THE DARK HILLS

Dark hills at evening in the west,
Where sunset hovers like a sound
Of golden horns that sang to rest
Old bones of warriors under ground,
Far now from all the bannered ways
Where flash the legions of the sun,
You fade—as if the last of days
Were fading, and all wars were done.

This poem is famously quoted by Robert Frost at the end of his introduction to one of Robinson's last books—where he focuses on the conditional phrase at the end, the "as if." Frost is making the point that Robinson, despite the sadness at the center of his poems, is always playful and always still seeking beauty out where it lies, despite what he knows. I think Frost is right on this score, but I also think he maybe undersells the complexity of the thing. I'm not sure that Robinson sees those endless wars as a sadness, per se, but a necessary part of the beauty in the first part of the poem. Or maybe necessary is the wrong word, he sees them as an unavoidable part of beauty. In short, one literally can't sing rightly of bobolinks and bees, to go back to that early quotation, if one doesn't also grasp the coming winter.

I love so much of how this little poem works, though. I love how we don't know it is an apostrophic poem until the seventh line. Up until that moment it feels like the poet is perhaps speaking directly to the reader—we are with him watching the sun light up the hills and he tells us what he sees.[2] Or more accurately, he tells us what he understands of what he sees. This short poem doesn't really have a lot of imagery (one of the criticisms often levelled at Robinson), but it has a lot of image-driven thinking. Look at how that first simile is such a synesthetic surprise—the sunset "hovers like a sound," and before the enjambment gives us the fallen warriors, we are hovering as well in the abstract wonder of this comparison.

When the line does turn, the poem deepens. It becomes a poem as much about time as it is about beauty. The "golden horns" and old warriors feel ancient here, from a past time, a place where honor and/or beauty may seem unimpeachable (Robinson often turned to old legends in his poems—see "Miniver Cheevy" for his take on this penchant of his), a time the dark hills watched over, saw the battles won, and which now fades into the distance. However the last line reminds us that the past does not exist without the present—and that our understanding of the past depends in ways on our awareness of the present. Those seemingly glorious battles of the past, were also violent and vicious, self-harming human tragedies. This poem, from the same book as "Song at Shannon's," was published in 1920, just after the first world war. Robinson, ever prescient in matters of human deficiency, knew that the war was neither glorious, or the end of anything. You can feel in the poem his fervent wish that it were so— that the beauty of those fading hills could be a kind of unquestioned faith in victory. But he knows better. And, despite that, he's made a beautiful poem about it. So, even with his characteristic realism (some might call it pessimism, but hey), beauty has won out in this poem.

Of course, it is an earned beauty—beauty with rough patches. Like the spondaic gestures that consistently interrupt the measured pace of the iambs in this poem ("Dark hills," "Old bones," "Far now," "You fade," "all wars"), Robinson seems to be saying that we can't understand or accept beauty without knowing its inevitably difficult context. So what am I suggesting here? That we let children see and hear the awful things of the world from the start? That we hit them so they should know pain? Of

---

2. Grammatically, the opening of the poem is ambiguous. What appears to be a dependent nominative clause turns out to be an address.

course not. Sheltering a child is an act of kindness, and protecting a child from physical and emotional harm is the duty of any parent. However, inculcating an awareness of difficulty, of complexity, of the presence of pain in the world, seems just as important. Maurice Sendak said in an interview once, "I refuse to cater to the bullshit of innocence"—and while that is certainly a strong way of phrasing what I'm after here, the sense is more or less right.[3] Or perhaps we need to rethink what we mean by innocent. All children, all people even, to some extent, are innocent. We did not ask to be created, and we are all figuring our way through a changing and confusing world. So what is imperative is that we not let our kids think we have everything figured out. And, in fact, there is no figuring it out. Isn't that what's at the heart of "Dark Hills"? That a romantic notion of honorable war is a lie—even the romantic notion of hills fading into the sunset is a lie. That sun will be back and it will be bright and brutal, and the wars, of course, will be back. So for a moment Robinson plays at understanding things—of getting beauty right—but then he gives up the game.

• • •

Rache has always been the most emotional of our three kids—and we've learned to just let the emotions come when they need to. He, like me, cries easily at a movie, and he'll get upset very quickly when things don't go his way. A few weeks ago we had to put down one of our dogs—she was fourteen and had been sick for many months at that point. It was an extremely sad ordeal, and leading up to the day the vet came to the house, any time Rache would ask if Ellie was going to be alright, I'd tell him that she probably would not be. He would almost immediately get upset and even slightly angry. But when the day finally came for her to go, and we asked the kids if they wanted to be inside or outside with Ellie, they all chose the latter, even Rache. Kate and I were surprised and a little trepidatious, but knew we had to let them make this choice themselves.

I had dug the grave for the dog that morning, and when we carried her empty body to the grave after the vet had gone, we were all crying—but I could sense in the kids a willingness, even readiness, to help and be a part

3. Interview in *The Guardian*, October 2, 2011

of Ellie's leaving us. And there was no romance in it—no feeling from any of us, least of all the kids, that this was a sad but beautiful family moment. This was not Robinson's ancient dark hills fading forevermore into the sunset. This was a reminder that loss is a permanent thing, and sure to revisit us. The kids were not just giving themselves over to one moment of loss, they were, consciously even I think, beginning a lifetime of loss and joy—bound up with one another so tightly you sometimes can't even feel the cracks. When Rache, on his own, headed to the shed to get our extra shovel to help put the dirt back in the hole I'd made, there were no "as ifs" in his mind, or mine, and we were closer to each other in sharing that hard fact.

• • •

I'd like to finish this thought on E.A. Robinson by considering two of his longer poems. I won't get to as much of either of them as I'd like, but I can only hold your attention for so long. The two poems are "Tasker Norcross" and "Avon's Harvest," the former from the same book as the other two poems we've looked at and the latter was published just a year later, in 1921, as a small book in its own right. Though written in blank verse, both poems are modernist masterpieces—investigating the terrifying holes inside human beings and the ways those holes, if left unchecked, will eat us from the inside. "Tasker Norcross" tells the story, more or less in the third person, of a man who cannot act, whose every day was a study of ineffectiveness and loneliness, a knowledge of too much, where "Avon's Harvest" is a story of hate—a cautionary tale of how lifelong hatred of another will inevitably destroy the hater with acid remorselessness. Both poems, then, are studies of another's life. Both poems also share the same dramatic situation—a listener/poet figure is told the story of the poem by another character—so both poems come to us not as tales told in the moment, but as records of listening and trying to understand, empathic objects in and of themselves.

Here's a passage from "Tasker Norcross:"

> *Blessed are they*
> *That see themselves for what they never were*
> *Or were to be, and are, for their defect*

At ease with mirrors and the dim remarks
That pass their tranquil ears.

And later, after describing the pale coldness of Norcross' house the narrator tells the poet/listener:

And hold the man before you in his house
As if he were a white rat in a box,
And one that knew himself to be no other.
I tell you twice that he knew all about it,
That you may not forget the worst of all
Our tragedies begin with what we know.

Here in Ferguson's telling (Ferguson is the name of the character telling the story), Norcross is a man who sees himself for what he is, and he is implicitly not "at ease" with mirrors, repelled instead by what he finds there. He is a man who grasps his own emptiness, the pain and terror of existing, and is rendered almost motionless by it—he cannot function in the world. In facing the binding of joy and pain, he can only see the pain. By the end of the poem Robinson makes it clear that no man named Tasker Norcross existed, and that Ferguson was talking, to his ostensible friend the poet/listener figure, about himself. In this psychological twist, the poem ceases to be a sort of sideshow freak exploration of a bizarre character, Norcross, and instead becomes a kind of condemnation of the poet/listener himself, and, by extension, the reader. If this listening friend had been able to see what Ferguson was doing, had been able to see Ferguson and reach more into the space between them, to do better than the mirror, he may have been able to cross some of the vast gulf that was isolating the "Norcross" of the narration from the rest of humanity. This poem is a warning—we must not merely listen to each other, but we must listen actively, with our hearts attuned as much as our ears.

While I do not think I'll share this poem yet with Rache (I can't even usually get my college students to read it), the lesson at the heart of it is a stark one for a parent. To be able to imagine the life of another is crucial—as crucial as being able to imagine one's own life. The poet/listener in the poem learnt too late of Norcross' true identity, too late to help Ferguson that is. But as parents, we must try to find ways to listen actively to the lives our kids describe to us. It's a little bit like the cans-and-string that were a sort of ubiquitous symbol of childhood communication in the pre-digital era (did that contraption ever actually work?). Both cans have to be held—there needs to be a can on either end for any kind of message to exist. While we may not always be able to understand what our kids, or any other people, are saying to us—in words or in actions—we need to find ways to at least hold the other can.

If we drop it, or don't teach our kids how to hold onto it—if they let the spaces grow, they create the opportunity for hate. And not hate like when my girls say they "hate" spinach, of course, but hate as a looming presence, hate as an inscrutable tumor inside and between us. Near the beginning of "Avon's Harvest,"[4] Robinson's long meditation on the effects of hate, as the poet/listener in this poem ponders how to get Avon to talk to him, he gives us this:

So many a time had I been on the edge,
And off again of a foremeasured fall
Into the darkness and discomfiture
Of his oblique rebuff, that finally
My silence honored his, holding itself
Away from a gratuitous intrusion
That likely would have widened a new distance
Already wide enough, if not so new.

Here Robinson speaks almost in the language of my little essay here. The poet/listener is afraid of falling into the "darkness" that is between them, that is always there between two people, and is only able to avoid it by truly listening—by offering an honorable silence which will not widen the distance that exists between them. Note that Robinson does not say it will close the distance, just keep it from getting worse. Avon then proceeds to tell the listener a long story of a held grudge—a hate that, over

4. There is also a strong element in this poem of the repressed homosexuality of the speaker Avon. In this reading, his hate for his former schoolmate becomes certainly also a hate for himself, an unwillingness to come to terms with his identity, but the impact of harboring that hate remains the same.

time, transformed itself into an all-consuming fear. At the end of the poem Avon dies from this fear (or from a ghost attack, depending on how you read it. . . .). Here is a curt summary from the poem itself of Avon's relationship with his own hate:

> *Beware of hate*
> *That has no other boundary than the grave*
> *Made for it, or for ourselves.*

So I suppose this, then, is the danger of my not fully imagining Rache's individual life (or his not learning to do the same). I'm not worried I will come to hate him, of course, but if I can't model things for him, guide him into the habit of such imagining, then the possibility of Avon's fate remains open to him.

As I was thinking about wrapping up this essay with this long weird poem, I read in the news this morning of a reelection rally President Trump held in North Carolina. Earlier this week he tweeted out a number of racist comments about a group of young congresswomen of color, telling them to "go back where they came from." At the rally, his supporters began to chant "send her back," in reference to one representative in particular who is Somali-American. Watching videos of these people chanting, spittle flying from their mouths, arms pumping threateningly along with the rhythm of the chant, I couldn't help but think of Avon. Somewhere in these people is a hate. Somewhere along the line they stopped trying to imagine the lives of other people and, as a result, are no longer able, even, to imagine their own lives. The hate in them, whether it be specific, as with Avon, or generalized, is what is widening the distances between them and others, between me and them—it is becoming boundaryless.

Of course, and finally, what Avon's hate turns into in the poem is fear. And that is what I saw in that rally crowd as well—fear masquerading as certainty, as belief. What I want more than anything for Rache, for all my kids, is to never feel that certainty, to never be completely sure they have something or someone else figured out. I would like them to be willing to extend their honorable silences to anyone, to their neighbors and friends, to the people at that rally, to strangers, to people they read about. The act of imagining another's life, as Robinson did so beautifully across his whole career, prepares us for those silences—it gives us a chance at honoring others' humanity. And more than anything, it keeps hate at bay. When Rache rides his bike into the hazy distance of a summer day, I am beginning to trust him, I'm imagining him trusting himself, I'm imagining him coming to love the dark lonely world he's riding through. He's measuring the distance between us, between him and everyone else, as if half-seriously considering a jump.

Dreamery Dreamer

Belle Randall and our Imaginations
(2020)

Who knows where we'll be when this last essay finds its way into print? It is one of the funny time-machine characteristics of writing—we can trim and tidy just before publication, but, in the end, everyone in on the bargain—reader and writer and publisher—knows that what looks current (black marks on a page in the hand) often comes from the past. And in this particular past—my current present—I am stuck in my bedroom waiting to find out if I test positive for COVID-19. I have a mild fever and no other real symptoms, but the fever is growing and I have a family. So, like a teenager holed up in his adolescent cave (like my almost-teenager Rache), I'm stuck in my room, or maybe, like a younger kid facing the music for a daily indiscretion, I've been sent to my room.

And what will I do here other than tamp down small-time panic fires? I'll read certainly and talk to my wife through the door and look at my kids about twenty feet away downstairs and try to keep the dog out of the room. I'll attend to the privileged tediousness of work; I'll write. But it occurs to me that all of those things require really just one skill—using the imagination. Now I'm not going to go all EPCOT on you here with that purple dragony thing I remember from my childhood (and Eric Idle spraying something at me in a ride?) or drag Wallace Stevens's private deity into this thing, but I want to think about how crucial our imaginations are for both survival and for art (and there's a way in which those two things aren't that different).

Right now I can hear my kids, after completing an hours-long bender on devices on this 100+ degree day (we're no parent-saints around here) gathering together a specific group of beloved stuffed animals to put on a play. These animals—known collectively as The Murphys—play an out-sized role in our family life. Few situations arise in which some member of the Murphy crowd is not referenced, and few movies or shows are watched when we don't debate which Murphy would play which role, whether it be the moralistic leader, Murphy, the greedy nemesis/uncle Butt, the hapless cloned brothers Tootington and Twoington, the spoiled child Floom, the evil baby Shemeniah, the extra-innocent ex-Cabbage Patch doll José or any of the other vast array of characters who figure into what began as a game but has by now become a kind of diamond-cut imaginative framework for understanding the world.

It strikes me as I listen to this survival work going on below me, while quarantining in my own panic-bunker, just how crucial imagination is for us in understanding the world and in bringing that understanding across to others. You know by now that I'm going to turn to poetry, of course, and I'm hoping that this final example will not be giving us any kind of *specific* guidance in how to be, be ourselves or be parents, but instead sort of what the stakes are in our being creative in a hard world. To do this I want us to look at the west coast poet Belle Randall. Randall made an impressive debut in the early 1970s with her book *101 Different Ways of Playing Solitaire*, which may well be in the top ten of first books by American poets. After that book, she spent decades publishing only small chapbooks (two in such small editions that I had to contact the bookmaker himself to find them) and published one other full length in the 2010s. An early poem, "A Child's Garden of Gods," has been anthologized, but otherwise her name and work seem significantly under-represented in the poetry landscape.

My readers won't be surprised to discover that Randall is a master of form (she studied with Thom Gunn in her young days), but she combines this formal acumen with a completely original noir-Americana aesthetic. She is sort of like Gjertrud Schnackenberg mixed with early Tom Waits. While one is liable to find in Randall's work philosophical sonnets or rhymed quatrains on the spiritual life, those are likely too to be shot through with cigarettes, Chinatowns, hood ornaments, liquor, smart shoes, and more. In short, as I read through her entire career, and she is one of those poets with whom one can spend a long afternoon completing the task, what I find is an imagination like no other I know in contemporary American poetry. Her poems are often in the third person, or are dramatic monologues from one-off characters, and they simply radiate with detail and precision. Here is an excellent, and gorgeously bizarre, example from that first book:

GENTLEMEN, THE BICYCLES ARE COMING!

Gentlemen, the bicycles are coming!
In silver, slanting rows like rain
They ride the moonlit highways toward
The towns where we lie dreaming.

Beyond the icy windowpane
As if a tuning fork were striking stars
We hear a spray of tiny bells
Cold, metallic, ringing,

And pushing back the curtains see
Stainless-steel handlebars
Like skeletons of scavengers
Upon us in the darkness winging.

There is a shaft of freezing air;
A moment when their headlights shine
Into our eyes; the bedroom walls
Are white, electrified, and gleaming.

The bicycles come sweeping down
The asphalt slope in starlit columns,
Pass the house and dwindle to
A flash of faint italics leaning

Round a distant curve, and Gentlemen—
They're gone! The curtains close,
And darkness spills across the shelves
Whose books, like tombs, contain their meaning.

What a marvelous poem. First, we can marvel at its formal ingenuity—only the last line of each stanza rhymes, rhyming as much with their repeated extra syllable (-ing) as with the root word (one thinks of Robinson's poem "Eros Turranos" perhaps), but the language is so musical throughout that the poem is still nearly songlike. There are one-off rhymes (the fork-struck "stars" with the threatening "handlebars") and moments of intense alliteration ("skeletons of scavengers") in addition to the recurring fourth line, and then there is the musical fealty to tetrameter (the meter of songs and nursery rhymes) which adds to the whimsical, and potentially not-so-whimsical, overall effect. But beyond these formal riches, the poem is a curious one. We never know who the eponymous "Gentlemen" are, and as such we don't know, really, who *we* are in the poem. Much less the speaker. As in much of the best of dramatic verse, we are dropped into the middle of a scene and are meant to make of the scene what we can with what we have. And what we have is simply spectacularly imagined observation. The cyclists come at us like the horsemen of the apocalypse updated, in tight formation, in "silver, slanting rows like rain." So, in that first simile, we are to see their coming as something not altogether unexpected, but also perhaps as something not entirely desirable.

So this poem of ominous arrival, of the observer trapped in the dark house "pushing back the curtains" cannot help but put me in mind of our situation here in these years stained by the pandemic, many of us in our houses for the nth consecutive month, trying to keep our children safe and happy, wondering what's coming and when. We can feel the fear in the speaker's voice, those "skeletons," the blinding headlights in the eye, the bedroom violated, and our imaginations similarly can run us to panic in this moment. As I sit here in my room awaiting my COVID test result, how can I keep from imagining the thing we don't want rushing at me down the hill, with a maddeningly curt bell announcing its arrival? But perhaps Randall gives us a trick here—we can't avoid the things that will come for us, but we can watch them when they do and retain our power of imagination and observation over them. Perhaps these bicycle men in the poem are unshrouded in a way by the careful, though terrified, description. We can't imagine things away, but we can reimagine them.

And by the end of the poem, the cyclists simply sweep past the house. In a sudden rush they become typescript on the page of the dark night (that incredible metaphor of the riders *as italics*) and the speaker is left back in her darkness, at least semi-content. Is there maybe a slight wistfulness in that final stanza? That the speaker maybe was hoping some-

thing would be exposed? Maybe. Maybe that's how it is with all things
that come to us through our imagination. Something arrives, we change
it, it changes us, and when it leaves we are a little confused. I sense that
here in the final line of the poem. Though frightening, the cyclists have
represented a kind of terrifying truth that the speaker has tried her best
to understand, but in the end could only guess at. And maybe that's the
best we can do.

Of course, a few days after I was thinking on this poem, the bicycle
bell, my phone, did ring for me, and I found out I had tested negative. A
lucky break, but also somehow even more mysterious. I wouldn't want to
have tested positive anymore than the speaker of the poem wants those
cycle lights in her house. But I certainly don't know much more than I
did or feel safer. But maybe I feel a bit more comfortable, or at least comforted, when I imagine whatever danger we might be in.

· · ·

One of the strangest things for me during this time of isolation and concern, and here, of course, I mean the period that began in March 2020
and, as of this writing in the summer of 2020, is continuing apace, has
been the natural world's complete lack of concern for our predicament.
Leaving aside any room for omens or prophecies, what I mean of course is
that everything went, and is going, on as it does—in April spring came in
on bright green wings; the dogwoods lit their sooty little matches in the
woods, the blackberries and blueberries flowered and set fruit. During
our home-staying we've gone out to the field to watch a supermoon rise,
kept tabs on a beehive in a nearby oak, watched the little groundhog on
the corner get fatter and funnier, saw a comet that must have dripped
from the bowl's-edge of the big dipper and heard the cicadas, as they do,
slowly tune in through the wide static of July.

It could be disconcerting to see the world so unconcerned, or it could
give one hope—it depends on the way the imagination processes what it
sees, I suppose. Personally, I see both things in the world; for me its lack
of concern is what gives me hope, and so I like to imagine it that way. The
dogwoods have nothing to do with me, so I was free to enjoy them. The
blackberries are mine, but also not mine; they are simply there. When
a hawk took two chickens in two days, it was not concerned with our
sadness. What perhaps we see in all of this, at least in a post-Romantic

worldview, is that it is very hard for us to look at the natural world without imbuing our observation with some kind of emotion or without wanting an emotional connection which might not be there. Enter the imagination:

SHE RIDES THE RUNNING BOARD OF DEATH

Why does she think of angels when she sees
A Ford sedan, round-fendered swell

Of 1942, abandoned now,
An empty shell, beneath the willow trees

And she a mother now herself, herself
An old and used machine whose offspring climbs

The windshield dark with morning-glory vines,
Tugs the glove compartment door and finds

A carcass hid where something green unwinds—
O egg from which an awful darkness pours,

Antique machine, engine green with moss—
This rattletrap is windowless. Dangling

Like a crucifix above the dash, a spider
Hangs, his web, like shattered glass, a pane

The butterfly escapes on winking wings.

What a lovely and strange poem. I imagine us in some kind of junkyard, or in the weeds of a front yard we've just passed by (or I'm lost in Janisse Ray's wonderful memoir). All you have to do is google images of a 1942 Ford sedan to get confirmation that this is exactly the car you think it is—round and shiny like a healthy face, neat tires, wide doors that look like they could have gangsters spilling out of them with Tommy Guns and crisp facial hair, and, of course, running boards. And this poem comes from a tiny chapbook of Randall's called *The Orpheus Sedan*, so the car is a bit of a theme or guiding image for her. But thinking of this poem, in particular, and nature's ambivalence to us and our imaginings, we see the car (and the woman in the poem) losing a slow war with time. The woman opens the poem by imagining angels, and we are then catapulted into Randall's take on the natural world overcoming this human thing, or all human things.

One of the things I like best about this poem is the way in which nature is kind of creepy in it. It puts one in mind of a poem like Robert Frost's "Design," and not just because of the shared spider imagery. Where the natural world in some poems might be a source of metaphorical comfort—an assurance of return or higher plans, here, instead, nature is frightening because it has no recognizable need or emotional driver, other than simply being. And whatever plans it might have do not involve us. Just like those COVID-era dogwoods outside my window, the vines climb the window of this car and slowly shut the light out, without knowing or caring.

Of course, Randall doesn't leave it at that—the poem is shot through too with spiritual imagery. We began with that angel, and we end with one too. That absolutely fantastic "winking" butterfly who escapes from the "pane" given to us by the marvelous homophonic line break. If the poem begrudges the reader an emotional connection to nature, it perhaps gives us a narrative one in that final image. All of this is to say that in this instance, Randall gives us a character, the woman from the title, who is riding just on the edge of despair. And in the world around her she sees both a disinterest in her, and a kind of endless hope. Maybe that is what we see in the world around us in this moment too. While there are still hurricanes and predators and diseases and choking vines, there are also moments of ephemeral beauty which somehow conquer all of that in their brevity. Or at least that is how I imagine it.

And I suppose, in my present-day reading of this poem, I have to see us as this beleaguered mother. We see in the car a good thing gone to disrepair; we see the inevitable failing of human ventures. Perhaps, to drag Frost back in here again, one might think of "The Woodpile" and its condemnation of the flightiness of human endeavor, but I think this poem is more openly sad, less judgmental. Also, importantly, there is that butterfly who escapes the jagged crucifix. I have left aside the obvious

religious reading of this poem (I'll let you handle that)—but it is important maybe to think of the ways this poem points out to the reader how
difficult it can be to find comfort in a hard time. I know from my family's
experience during this crisis, and from reading about others' experiences,
that depression and sadness and anxiety of all kinds are flourishing in
the present uncertainty, flourishing like the vines climbing up that old
sedan. And when we turn to our usual sources of comfort—friends, religion, learning, television, cocktails, you name it—they might seem lesser,
or less able, at least, to help us. The sedan in the poem was at one point a
symbol of freedom, conqueror of the great American road, but now it is
stuck in time's endless coda. I think I can relate to that feeling. Though
Randall does not give her protagonist any real way through the cloud of
her sadness, she does give her, and the child in the poem, that butterfly, a
briefly glimpsed (or perhaps only imagined) moment of beauty. And that
will have to be enough for us as well.

. . .

Along with the dispassion of the natural world, another fact that will stick
with me from this time of crisis is a feeling that we, at least as a collective
American whole, are somewhat incompetent. Or at least, it turns out,
incapable of working together, truly together, to solve a larger problem.
(Maybe this is one problem the natural world does not have.) There are
certainly elements of political failure in our case—a refusal of the government to spearhead a collective response to this pandemic—but turning
to politics will just make me sadder right now. Because really, the political failure seems to me as much a symptom of the individual, intimate
imaginative failure of each of us as anything else. And it's not so much a
lack of imagination that I am blaming here but a failure of it—a misuse of
its powers I suppose. From the beginning of this country to some extent,
though more so since the reactionary eighties to now, there has been an
insistence that the imagined individual, with all of their walls and powers and weapons and rights, is the ultimate vision of an American. That,
essentially, we exist in order to defend, and then dote on, our own bodies
only. Of course, this fantastical vision ignores the simple fact that we are
primates, and primates don't act as individuals. As Robert Yerkes, the pri-
matologist, put it: "One chimpanzee is no chimpanzee." That is true for
us as well.

So when we imagine ourselves as inviolable single entities, we are using one of the things that makes us human—the imagination—to dehumanize ourselves. Impressive. We could blame a Judeo/Christian worldview (the idea of just an Adam and an Eve is just too un-monkeyish to be credible), or we could blame the Enlightenment (though to some extent we'd need to blame a partial misreading of the Enlightenment), but I think it is safer just to blame ourselves. By spending so much time imagining ourselves, we have let atrophy the ability, or willingness, to imagine others as part of ourselves. Primates don't just think of themselves as members of a community, they think of the community, their community, as an integral part of themselves. This is a very different concept of the individual than the one America has been harping on about for so long now. This is why when you pay taxes, you are meant to understand that the municipal good *is* your good. This is why when a fire is put out across town it keeps you safe as well. This is why inequality harms the rich as much as the poor. We are all of us enmeshed in each other.

Here's Belle Randall with a sarcastic take on this situation. This is a sonnet from a handmade chapbook from the 1990s, *True Love*:

SALAD DAYS

We were the last of the great dinosaurs,
remember? Held by monsoon summers that
were warm inside like women or old caves,
we loved ourselves, and, being fat, thought that
the only way to be. We waddled through
manure smells to swamp's edge and sat,
two stupendous babies, swaddled to
our bellies in the mud. Your lovely rump
was green with scales like leaves of artichoke
and if you accidentally plumped it on
the children of some small-limbed vertebrate—
that's why they call it crude. We liked a joke,
cold-blooded as we were. We had our rights,
our way of life, our yawning appetites.

So here we stand ("like an Adam and an Eve" as David Byrne sang) as prelapsarian dinosaurs in Randall's capacious imagination. I can't help but think here of that sitcom from the early nineties which featured a family of anthropomorphic dinosaur puppets (does anyone but me remember that? Was I dreaming?), and this poem has something of comedy in it, or at least of a biting satire. What of course is looming is extinction. I'm not sure I've ever thought of the Christian fall as a kind of extinction event—but here Randall imagines our complacency and arrogance as being fully self-defeating. Kind of makes the present day feel even more calamitous.

There are so many moments in this sonnet to admire—the way the dinosaurs are faux-innocents, "two stupendous babies" who "waddle through" the cartoonish landscape. Though they are not innocent of course, they crush the things in their way and are focused, as we are, on "[their] rights." Normally I find the English sonnet form to be less supple than its Italian counterpart—the couplet of the former providing too neat a conclusion compared to the wildly open sestet of the latter. But in this bitter little moment, the couplet is just right. Can anyone think of a better pair of words to be yoked by rhyme than "rights" and "appetites?" I'll wait while you think of one.

OK. And let us not, before we move on, ignore the marvelous opening of the poem. The wet climate of this place that is "warm inside like women" where "we loved ourselves." This moment is so simply put and yet so devastating. The simile adds a bit of lewdness to the poem (and in this entire chapbook, Randall has an earthy erotic touch) which makes the comment that we "loved ourselves" have an overtone we may not have otherwise heard. In short, these proto-people to me feel fully imagined on the page. We immediately see ourselves in these cartoons and feel both playfully and terribly judged. So the imagination here is revealed as not just a plaything, not just a survival tool to keep us engaged positively with the world, the natural world, etc., but also as a tool that can teach us hard truths about ourselves and the systems in which we are complicit.

• • •

So, we've thought now about the imagination as a means of making fear a more intimate and comfortable thing, how it helps us perhaps begin to observe the steady uncaring and beautiful stories of the natural world told alongside our stories, and how we abuse the imagination in conceiving of ourselves; and Randall's poems have provided remarkable signposts. Let's look at one more example, this time one that perhaps gives us some hope. Here's the second section of a poem called "The Pawnbroker" from Randall's most recent book, *The Coast Starlight* (2010):

I'm Sol
of Solomon & Sons.
Through my soiled hands

Pass a second time
the family jewels and bone,
ancient china plate and platter—

Pattern in dense rows,
The richness of my stores, my own
fly-specked windows hung

With fishing rods, dinner jackets, guns,
Nikon cameras, triple tier
blue glitter drums;

My name a scroll
on glass crossed and double-crossed
with wire; the light broken

On the squinting grin
of the unlikely kid—
the day's first customer—

Wanting in.
        Come in, come in,
                young dreamery dreamer.

What brings you to my gate
with its padlock, the leaden clock
whose combination I unlock?

What yen, what hot
pearl beyond all price to hock?
Should I lift

A battered trumpet from
the overhanging rows, or break
a saxophone and place

Each member in the blood-
red velvet-lined
coffin of its case?

Come in, come in,
young second-hand schemer.
I juggle with

Not much,
three balls: the sign
of the redeemer.

To some extent we are all the kid in this poem, the young "schemer" coming to the pawn shop to see what's what. But we might also be Sol, the god-like owner of the shop who seems to have almost stepped out of a Tom Waits song (I told you he was in here). Who among us couldn't describe their life like this—as a collection of random objects, forgotten mementos, fragments shored against their ruins, etc. Perhaps one of the most characteristic, almost talismanic, entities in my time as a parent has been the small or medium-sized buckets of assorted toys that seem to pop up all over the house. I dump out a small witches' cauldron and find three or four plastic animals, a few markers, a granola bar wrapper, three dimes, doll pants and a comb. A cracked Tupperware bottom under Lois's bed holds a broken watch, the butt-end of a plastic recorder, a superhero's leg, something fuzzy, a small chair made of cardboard and tape, a clay turtle, and one sock. Inevitably, if I move to throw most of these things away, as if they were alerted by some kind of inner warning system, one of the kids arrives over my shoulder to sort through the detritus and find what needs to be kept. If for some reason, I manage to throw it all away without being caught, within hours someone will ask me if I've seen a particular item that was almost certainly in the cauldron.

Randall's imagination in "The Pawnbroker" understands and encompasses my kids' imaginations. My favorite thing about this poem, beyond the amazing ear-wormy subtle rhyming, is just the things in it. I love the dinner jackets; I love the bone plates, the padlock like a clock, the double-crossed glass, and most of all I love that saxophone—the incredible way it is broken and lovingly (terrifyingly?) put in its "blood-red" case. For my kids even the broken things in their lives have value, and it is hard to imagine any small thing as having out-lived entirely some purpose. That's the same impulse driving this poem—that maybe any seemingly spent or broken thing, any broken moment, spent promise, broken future, broken present can be redeemed. Though the pawnbroker in the poem, by the end, presents himself as a kind of jester (can we trust him?) we are grateful to him for simply offering us the chance at redemption.

As we wait out these broken days of the pandemic, a large-scale societal version of my being stuck in my room perhaps, I think we're going to have to use our imaginations to get out of it. So often my kids will say they're bored, or that there's "nothing to do"—but really, of course, they're just not flexing the right muscle. If I just ignore them, I know before too long they'll be off playing some just-imagined game, scripting the Murphys next adventure, or writing a story, or drawing, or reading. We are going to need to have that flexibility too. Can we dream our way out of this mess? Maybe, says Belle Randall, if we qualify what we mean by dream. If we dream that we can understand each other, if we dream that fear and contentment may sometimes come together, if we dream ourselves into the beautiful and forbidding world around us, if we dream that whole things might just mostly be made of broken things, perhaps.

And in that way perhaps I can dream too that these essays come together into some kind of whole—five years of watching my children move through the world; five years in which they have changed so much—Rache, Jane Bell, and Lois, all five years older and a thousand years grown up. I fear that I have changed very little: I wave away the same ghosts with my hands; I read the same poems; I wake up the same tired; I plan many of the same plans with my slightly more lined hands. But that's OK. If there is a whole, it's not the kind to hold in my hands. I'll put it in my heart even if no one knows it's there. I'll put it there with my interests. I'll put it there with my loves. I'll put it there with my patience, my cares, my doubts, my imperfections, my moonmen, my expectations, my pleasures, my purpose, my darkness, my selfishness and sympathies, my imagination, my kids, my wife, and also with my dreams.

Works Mentioned

Basbanes, Nicholas A. *Cross of Snow: A Life of Henry Wadsworth Longfellow*, Knopf, 2020

Bishop, Elizabeth. *Poems*, Farrar, Straus and Giroux, 2011

Bishop, Elizabeth. *Collected Poems*, Farrar, Straus and Giroux, 1983

Brooks, Gwendolyn. *Selected Poems*, Harper and Row, 1963

Brooks, Gwendolyn. *Blacks*, 1987 Third World Press, ninth printing, 2001

Byrne, David, "Nothing but Flowers," *Naked*, The Talking Heads, Sire Records, 1988

Coatsworth, Elizabeth. *Fox Footprints*, Knopf, 1923

Coatsworth, Elizabeth. *Atlas and Beyond*, Harper & Brothers, 1924

Coatsworth, Elizabeth. *Compass Rose*, Coward-McCann, 1929

Coatsworth, Elizabeth. *Country Poems*, Macmillan, 1942

Donaldson, Scott. *Edwin Arlington Robinson: A Poet's Life*, Columbia, 2007

Evernden, Neil. "Beyond Ecology: Self, Place, & the Pathetic Fallacy." *The Ecocriticism Reader: Landmarks in Literary Ecology*, ed. Cheryll Glotfelty and Harold Fromm. University of Georgia, 1996

Frost, Robert. "Introduction," *King Jasper: A Poem* by Edwin Arlington Robinson. Macmillan, 1935

Frost, Robert. *Collected Poems, Prose, and Plays*, Library of America, 1995

Hayden, Robert. *Collected Poems*, Liveright, 1985

Hill, Geoffrey. *Broken Hierarchies: Poems 1952–2012*, ed. Kenneth Haynes, Oxford University Press, 2013

Hollis, Matthew. *Now All Roads Lead to France: A Life of Edward Thomas*, W.W. Norton, 2011

Keats, John. *Letters of John Keats*, ed. Robert Gittings, Oxford University Press, 1970

Lerner, Ben. *The Hatred of Poetry*, Farrar, Straus and Giroux, 2016

Longfellow, Henry Wadsworth. *Poems and Other Writings*, ed. J. D. McClatchy. Library of America, 2000

Melville, Herman. *Moby-Dick; or, The Whale*, Harper, 1851

Muir, Edwin. "Poetry and the Poet," *The Estate of Poetry*, Harvard University Press, 1962

Randall, Belle. *101 Different Ways of Playing Solitaire, and Other Poems*, University of Pittsburgh Press, 1973

Randall, Belle. *The Orpheus Sedan*, Copper Canyon Press, 1980

Randall, Belle. *True Love*, Wood Works, 2003.

Randall, Belle. *The Coast Starlight*, David Roberts Books, 2010

Ransom, John Crowe. *Selected Poems*, third edition, Knopf, 1991

Ray, Janisse. *Ecology of a Cracker Childhood*, Milkweed, 1999

Robinson, E.A. *The Three Taverns*, Macmillan, 1920

Robinson, E.A. *Avon's Harvest*, Macmillan, 1921

Scarbrough, George. *Tellico Blue*, E. P. Dutton, 1949

Scarbrough, George. *Summer So-Called*, E. P. Dutton, 1956

St. John, Primus. *Communion: New and Selected Poems*. Copper Canyon Press, 1999

Thomas, Edward. *The Collected Poems of Edward Thomas*, ed. R. George Thomas, Oxford University Press, 1981

Wonder, Stevie. *Innervisions*, Motown Records, 1973